the

HOW

to

INNER
PEACE

A Guide to a New Way of Living

the

HOW

to

INNER
PEACE

A Guide to a New Way of Living

CONSTANCE KELLOUGH

books that change your life

namaste

PUBLISHING

VANCOUVER, CANADA

ISBN 978-1-897238-97-4

Library and Archives Canada Cataloguing in Publication

Title: The how to inner peace : a guide to a new way of living / Constance Kellough.
Names: Kellough, Constance, 1947- author.
Description: Includes bibliographical references and index.
Identifiers: Canadiana 20200294709 | ISBN 9781897238974 (softcover)
Subjects: LCSH: Peace of mind. | LCSH: Meditation.
Classification: LCC BF637.P3 K45 2021 | DDC 158.1/2—dc23

Note: Excerpts of this book have been taken from a previous book published by the same
author: *The Leap – Are You Ready to Live a New Reality?*

This book is meant to be informative, not prescriptive. The author of this book does not
dispense medical advice nor prescribe the use of any technique or practice as a form of
treatment for physical, mental, emotional, or medical problems, without the advice of a
qualified physician, either directly or indirectly. The intent of the author is only to offer
information of a general nature to help you in your quest for emotional and spiritual
well-being. In the event that you use any of the information in this book for yourself or
another, the author and the publisher assume no responsibility for your actions and their
consequences.

Published by:

NAMASTE PUBLISHING
P.O. Box 72073, Vancouver, BC, Canada V6R 4P2
www.namastepublishing.com

Distributed in North America by: Ingram/Publisher's Group West
Cover and interior book design: Mary Kellough

Printed in Canada on recycled paper by
FRIESENS CORPORATION

DEDICATION

To the Spirit within all of us

NOTE TO THE READER

Do not practice any form of meditation, including Innerbody Meditation, while you are driving, working with machinery or in situations requiring mental alertness.

CONTENTS

1

BEFORE WE BEGIN

Written intentionally in a sequenced manner, *The HOW to Inner Peace* is not intended to be a quick mental read but something that more importantly is intended to speak to your heart and spirit so as to evoke a greater experience of inner peace.

I suggest you read it for the first time from beginning to end. Then, read it a second time, this time sensing its content with your whole body. Pause after each chapter or even after each section within a chapter and integrate the content, not only at the level of mental comprehension but also on the vibrational consciousness and heart levels. These pauses could be for a minute or several, an hour, or even a number of days—the frequency and length of each pause to be determined intuitively by you.

Throughout this book you will find spiritual practices within the context of a particular chapter or at the end of one or a subsection within it. These spiritual practices are to encourage and support you to more readily integrate the text and through reflection and action assist you to move step-by-step toward what for many of us is a new *felt experience* – inner peace. You may find yourself wanting to stay with a certain practice for some time before continuing to read and moving on to the next. Or you may find you are drawn to certain practices that you want to revisit again and again so as to integrate them into your life.

On your first read through this book, questions may arise for you at certain points. Please continue reading and see if you get a better understanding, answer, or confirmation later in the book. In addition, at times I introduce a teaching, a point, or words such as "stillness", "acceptance", "Inner Knower", and "inner body" that I elaborate on later in the book.

Questions such as what is consciousness, the ego, and your essence have been answered in many ways and are hard to define simply because they are not things that can be grasped by our physical senses or the thinking mind. Nor can all things be explained through logic or science. Yet, such intangibles are very real.

Because there are truths beyond verification through intellect and scientific findings, when reading this book, you will need to rely on your spiritual understanding and personal experiences to determine what is helpful and felt truth for you at this time.

Others may have their own views on what I present in this book. My sharing is based on my truth as I have come to know it through many years steeped in meditation; spiritual inquiry, reading, and practice; teaching and publishing within the genres of body/mind/spirit – but more importantly, through *personal experience*.

You can't know anything for certain other than what you have personally experienced – mentally, emotionally, physically, spiritually. You don't have to have faith when you have personal experience. That is why this book is purposely written to be experiential for the reader.

You may find repetition as you read on. This is purposeful. It is for reinforcement and to present certain teachings in other contexts. Additionally, throughout this book, "Self", "One Self", "true Self", "Divine Self" are used synonymously, as are "Source" and "Divine Source". I intuitively felt which wording to use in specific contexts.

Because the purpose of this book is to bring about inner awareness, I refer only to the science and mind knowledge that is necessary to substantiate parts of the text.

Let us begin.

2

THE WAY FORWARD

"Once you choose hope, anything is possible."

Christopher Reeves

HOPE

Hope is not based on belief. It is a strong energy that comes from our heart. It holds to an optimistic state of mind with the expectation of positive outcomes. When we have hope, we also trust, trust that love will win out because it is the only true power. With hope and trust, doubt and resistance cannot survive. What remains is inner peace. Those who have hope are lovers of Life who bring their concern and love to all of humanity and all living things. Love is the causative factor that never fails. Just as compassion is ineffectual if it is not followed by action - if only the action is a silent blessing or prayer - hope requires us to take action. But because of the principle: "As within so without", the action we first need to take is to go within, get in touch with our inner being and thereby grow to a higher consciousness of love and caring that will then emanate out and touch others.

HOPE IS MORE THAN JUSTIFIED

We are all well aware of the challenges of modern life and threats of global situations. These bear no repeating, especially at the beginning of this book. To do so may evoke more fear, and that is not what this book is about.

Every age and even every decade have their unique challenges. Yet humanity has continued to evolve. We are part of Mother Nature that has taught us co-existence, adaptation, resiliency, and regeneration. We have hope that at this time in our evolution as a species, humanity now has the ingenuity, intelligence, wisdom, and means to respond effectively to current challenging events and those that are likely predictable.

This book is about hope and, indeed, a personal felt certainty that if a sufficient number of us commit to living from a higher level of consciousness Now, we can and will have a spiritual renaissance. By opening our hearts to embrace all in our Oneness, we will experience a realization of our true Self. Sri Aurobindo, Indian philosopher, yogi, and guru (1872 – 1950) and his then contemporary Pierre Teilhard de Chardin, philosopher, Christian mystic, and Catholic priest (1881 – 1955), and the Christian Apostle Saint Paul all predicted this spiritual transition or awakening.

Such a shift to a higher level of consciousness will result in an increased level of global-wide caring. How can I have such hope? What grounds are there for believing that personally and collectively we will break free of our ages-long madness?

At the same time as we are seeing the insanity in our species that can no longer be hidden because of the access we have to vast and immediate information through new communication technologies, we are also witnessing an increase in the opposite polarity, one of a higher consciousness of responsibility and caring.

HOPE IN ACTION

We are experiencing a blossoming in the arts and other creative works. We are also seeing miraculous advances in the fields of science, medicine, and technology together with an accelerating movement pressing for a more egalitarian distribution of the world's resources, and an unstoppable movement to gender equality. Many individuals of great wealth are contributing generously to noble causes. People are increasingly demonstrating their concern for others by giving to causes they personally feel are important through vehicles such as crowdfunding.

There is an ever-increasing movement toward environmental responsibility, albeit we still have a long way to go to address environmental challenges. In growing numbers, people are doing what they can to help heal Mother Earth and prevent an acceleration of global warming. Just one example is what is being accomplished by 4oceans: At this time, 7,193,285 pounds of trash, especially plastics, have been removed from oceans and coastlines by their paid employees since 2017, and they invite all of us to participate in this endeavor.[1]

Pressure is mounting on multiple fronts, and often from the ground up, for the protection of human rights and the ending of repressive dictatorships because repressive forces are still evident in our world.

It is heartening to witness volunteerism in many countries. These volunteers include medical and other professionals who often, at their own expense, take time from their busy professional schedules to serve in developing countries. Who cannot smile with gratitude when we hear about such groups as Doctors Without Borders who volunteer though a licensed foundation to deliver life-saving services to those who cannot afford access to medical care. Other organizations providing assistance include Amnesty International that works to end the abuse of human rights throughout the world, and Global Witness whose mission is to expose corruption and environmental abuse. The list goes on and on, from charitable foundations dedicated to providing a healthy breakfast to underprivileged school children to those who save people from River Blindness in Nigeria.

Factfulness, a book by Hans Rosling, with Ola Rosling and Anna Rosling, presents many "good news" facts of how humanity has advanced. Hans Rosling was a medical doctor and professor of international health and adviser to the World Health Organization and UNICEF.

In his book, Rosling admits that the current state of the world is both bad and better, and has presented some of the better that we often don't hear about because the media is mainly trumpeting daily the fear-evoking events that get our attention, while the new global wide improvements are often slow to show the evidence of such and do not qualify as instant "breaking news".

Several of the improvements cited in *Factfulness* are: Extreme poverty, described as earning less than $2 per day has been reduced from 50% in 1966 (1.5 billion people of a 3 billion world population) to 9% in 2017 (684 million people of a 7.6 billion world population). Share of people with water from a protected source rose from 58% in 1980 to 88% in 2015. Oil spills of 1,000 tons from tanker ships went down from 636 in 1979 to 6 in 2016. Girls registered in primary schools rose to 90% in 2015 from 65% in 1970. If we look for them, the "good news" stories are there.

PRACTICE
Because we tend to see something when we intentionally look for it, during the next week, look for evidence of "good news" and make a mental or written note of such incidences.

PRACTICE
Because things we dwell on usually increase or intensify, make a list of all the positive things you are grateful for in your life – people, situations, your own personal strengths, gifts, and positive behaviors. How do you feel now?

Whenever you become discouraged, bring back this feeling.

PRACTICE
Whenever something "negative" happens in your experience, instead of giving into the impulse to react to it, resist it, challenge yourself to find some good in it, and dwell on that.

Of great importance, there is a new spiritual consciousness emerging that is broad-based, planet-wide, non-sectarian, and inclusive of all. This higher level of consciousness is based on the realization that humans are essentially spiritual beings whose true nature is rooted in love and who are all connected in Oneness.

Meditation has moved out of the realm of the mystical into everyday living. It is now being practiced not only by individuals in their homes but also in meditation centers, in some schools, and enlightened businesses. Meditation has spread to virtual groups connecting to meditate online. In addition, through the use of the internet, people are informed of when to sit in meditation for a specified purpose at a specific time in their own time zone. In this way we can participate in global wide focused meditations. This growing awareness of the importance of the practice of meditation and of being mindful in what we do is significant. When we sit in stillness or what has sometimes been referred to as "silent prayer", we are able to listen to the wisdom of the soul within us, which is conveyed not through words but through non-verbal awareness.

People are waking up to the need to do what they can to take positive, loving action in their lives. They realize that something must be done to break free of humankind's personal and global conflicts in order to turn our world around. While taking what action they can within their own current spheres of influence, now people are also tending to care globally because they have come to see how we are all connected, how inter-dependent we are, how one segment of humanity affects the whole.

THE NEED TO STEP UP OUR SPIRITUAL PRACTICES

I believe our survival as a species will be found in the realm of spirit. HOW can we make this necessary shift to a more spiritual-based existence?

Traditional spiritual practices will no longer suffice. Though many of the parliaments and churches of the world pray for peace, and people on every continent march for peace, the reality of external peace eludes us – because peace must first be found, be *experienced* within us. Even when we intensify the earnestness and frequency of our prayers, we inevitably experience a frustration in not getting the results we need *now* to stop further suffering, loss of lives, and destruction. A rapid personal healing and that of the divisions within our world will not come from simply continuing with our existing secular and spiritual practices. Humanity needs to step up its spiritual work.

THE NEED TO FIND OUT WHO WE TRULY ARE

If you are reading this now, I believe that, intuitively, no matter your age, you know we are a transition generation, the ones to bridge to a better world. As the Hopi Elders have so clearly reminded us, that at this time, we are not to look outside ourselves for our leaders since "We are the ones we have been waiting for." [2]

This book invites us to make an evolutionary shift – from egoic fear to felt Oneness.

The kind of shift this entails can be seen in *The Thin Red Line*, a movie about the realities of combat in the South Pacific during the Second World War. In one scene, a soldier is surveying a field after the battle of Guadalcanal. He is stunned by the grim carnage. Many of his comrades – some dead, some with gaping wounds, still others writhing in their limbless bodies in excruciating pain – are strewn on the ground like fodder for vultures.

Some pitch in to help the survivors, others stand or sit, stunned by the horror of what has just happened, their faces showing the shock at such insanity. As the narrating and witnessing soldier looks at his surviving comrades, he says, "Maybe we only have one big soul that everyone is a part of. Each face the same man—like one big Self. Each one looking for salvation on their own, like coals thrown from the fire." This soldier's words pierce to the heart of our human tragedy.

Our inability to solve our world's problems is due to our lack of understanding that we are all part of "one big Self." Instead, we are limited by our belief that we are each separate individuals: "pieces of coal thrown from the fire". It is this belief in separation that causes most of our non-rational based fears and the conflicts we experience on both the individual and collective levels.

When we come from "separation-thinking", we truly do not know who we are.

The Ancient Greeks were aware of the importance of self-awareness. The Oracle at Delphi, alleged to be a channel by a high priestess from the "god" Apollo, says, "KNOW THYSELF". The Greeks were told of the importance of the Oracle's message, but centuries later, most of humanity is still grappling with finding the answer to who they truly are. Is the difficulty in finding the answer because we don't know HOW to do this?

We cannot come into an awareness of who we truly are until we accept that as human beings we have a body and experience all aspects of being human in a body. However, more importantly, we are also spiritual beings, each having an individual soul. We cannot come into the awareness of who we truly are until we experience and live from the nature of our soul.

Some have already evolved in consciousness to be sufficiently aware of who they truly are. And when they came into this awareness, simultaneously they came to the awareness of the Oneness of their true Self. At this time, however, only a fraction of humanity has yet to come to this realization.

When you come into the realization of your true Self, that expresses itself through your individual form, you realize that the stillness, peace, love and joy within you are not exclusively yours. One cannot say "my peace" and "your peace": there is simply peace. Peace, joy, love are qualities of our true Self. They are unchanging, invisible and eternal. They cannot be threatened. These states of Being are accessible to all, only seeking our recognition through *felt experience*.

3

WHAT WE ARE NOT

Before we embark on the journey of finding out who we truly are, it is worth reminding ourselves what we are *not*.

LABELS

You are not your name. Your name was either given to you at birth or changed through marriage or personal decision. When we meet others, we normally say, "Hello, I am – followed by what you call yourself. "I am Susan Thompson," for example. But Susan Thompson is not who you are. It is just an identification label. More accurately, Susan could introduce herself by saying, "My name is Susan Thompson." This is a good practice for all of us.

We are not our titles such as Vice-President, Sales Manager, Chief Executive Officer, Head of Creative Design, Supervisor, Hair Stylist, Store Manager, Lawyer, Bus Driver, Doctor, Nurse, Teacher, Barista, Plumber. Those are what we currently do or titles that have been given to us by others based on level of education, training, skills, success, leadership capability, or the job position we hold. Yet how we often cling to our titles. The more we identify ourselves with titles, the more our titles become part of who we think we are. The greater the degree to which we are attached to our titles to give us an identity and self-worth, the more we fear the pain of losing them, and the more we box ourselves in and not open to the opportunities for expansion life brings to us.

ONLY THE PHYSICAL BODY

Reading the story of Narcissus through the eyes of spiritual awareness, we see that he fell into the illusion that his physical form was his ultimate reality. The external body and the external world are only passing forms, each of them transitory expressions of the ultimate reality of who we truly are. If we misidentify with the body and bodily experiences as our only reality, we ensure that fear will be our predominate state, not love.

We are not only the physical body. The body is a vehicle used to experience and learn in this lifetime. As *A Course in Miracles* tells us, the body's primary function is to be a means of communication, a means of connecting with one another, serving one another. When it has served its purpose, consciousness leaves it and only a lifeless corpse remains. If we identify ourselves only with our bodily form, we prevent ourselves from finding our true Self. We are so much more than our bodies.

Do not let your physical senses mislead you. It is the physical eyes of the body that look out and see separate selves and often only what they want to see or have been conditioned to see.

There is the recounted incident of a group of radiologists who were asked to look at an x-ray to see if they could find any evidence of cancer. Because they were trained to look for certain things, when looking at the x-ray, the vast majority of the group did not see the gorilla in the x-ray, which would have been readily seen by a layperson's eyes. Over and over again it comes to our attention that we tend to see what we are looking for, that we see what we expect to see, that we see what we have been conditioned to see.

We often make unfair assumptions and judgments with our outer senses, especially our sight. We move from *sensation* to *association* and then often to assumption. How often have we made instant assumptions about another or a situation based on our five outer senses alone and later found out our assumptions were completely false and not fair. It is painful when we act on some false assumption and then realize only too late that we were wrong. Mental assumptions based on outer senses are not to be confused, of course, with what our intuition and inner knowing tell us – like when we are not in a safe place or when it is time to let go of someone or some situation and get on with our life.

We have our five outer senses. These serve as tools for our experiences and bring in information from our immediate environment and the world. Our outer senses send electrical impulses to the brain: hot stove, high winds, old person, tastes sweet, angry face, and other things we take in through our outer senses. These are basic and primordial. We need our five senses to move safely and successfully in the world. Indeed, sensory deprivation can lead to depression or even a mental breakdown.

If we only believe and act on what we can perceive or prove through our five outer senses and use these sensations to make associations and link thoughts together and if we reject anything else as not valid, we are left with a limited and distorted understanding of reality. Then we can't see things on a non-physical or spiritual basis, things as they are beyond what can be known by the five outer senses and thinking mind – things as they are on a subtle, more conscious level.

Yes, I know. Our body screams out and says such things as, "I'm hungry. I am cold. My nerves are acting up. My throat is sore today. I was in a car accident last year that left my right arm paralyzed. I am afraid of crowds. I grieve for my deceased brother." All of this seems so real. And it is! On one level, of course, the body is real and our bodily experiences, whether painful, neutral, or pleasurable are real. They are manifestations of the human experience. But our body is not our ultimate reality.

If we are going to become unstuck from human pain, we will have to become unstuck not only from the problematic ego, but also from thinking our body and experiences we have in the body are all we are—while simultaneously not derogating the body in any way. The body is vitally important to our awaking to higher consciousness. It is the perfect form that enables us to have the experience of being human and to use our human experiences to move into the awareness of our spiritual nature.

PRACTICE
Ask yourself, "What would happen, would change if I no longer identified myself only as a body and the experiences of the body?" Sit in silence. Revisit the question. Note how your life would be different. Next, ask yourself, "How would I relate to others if

I no longer identified them as being only their body and bodily experiences?" Again, sit in silence then revisit the question. Note how you would relate to others differently.

ROLES WE PLAY

We are not the roles we play, such as mother, father, grandmother, sister, nephew, neighbor, friend, champion golfer, spiritual teacher, and so on. Yes, we take action in the world through these roles but the level of consciousness we bring to these actions usually determines how effective we are in them. It is wonderful to be a mother, husband, business leader, et cetera, but more importantly, what level of consciousness do we bring to the roles we play in our life? There are many books and workshops on The Conscious Leader, The Conscious Parent, The Conscious Teacher; however, a person can't be a Conscious Leader, for example, or be conscious in any role they play until they first become conscious of who they truly are. They will then bring this heightened awareness and higher vibration of consciousness into every relationship and everything they do.

WHAT IS CONSCIOUSNESS?

Firstly, consciousness isn't a thing, so it cannot be described like an object. Consciousness is all pervasive and itself is formless yet can also take form. It is the field that holds everything. All of creation is born of consciousness at different levels of vibration. Consciousness is our visible bodies, the invisible force and intelligence within our bodies, and the "glue" that connects us in Oneness. In modern day science, consciousness is now often being referred to as the "Field".

"The field is everything", said Einstein. He was referring to the unseen energy field in and around everything visible and non-visible. Everything is energy in vibration. Seemingly solid objects, including our bodies, are not solid at all. What appears as the dense form of our bodies is actually 99.9% space. In that space is vibrational energy.

Indeed, everything is made up of the energy of consciousness as vibration. Even though we can't see consciousness in its formless state, it is nevertheless there. For the most part, the more solid a thing and not exhibiting the life force of movement, the less consciousness resides within it, with one likely exception: the mineral kingdom. For example, some individuals claim certain precious and semi-precious stones in the mineral kingdom such as quartz crystal, amber, rose stone, amethyst, jade, and so on express a unique, vibrant, and helpful energy.

Although everything is made up of consciousness, there is more of the life force of consciousness in a live tree than there is in the wood of a chair, for example, more in a living flower than in a coffee cup – and immensely more consciousness within our living bodies.

Although we cannot see thought forms and emotional energies with our physical eyes, we know they exist because we *experience* them. Negative thoughts and emotions have a lower vibration of consciousness than positive thoughts and emotions.

Consciousness is causative. It creates. That is why we have been told to watch our thinking mind, which although troublesome at times, is still part of consciousness. Thoughts can create negative emotions, which then come back to us as negative things happening in our lives. The same process is true, of course, regarding positive thinking. This is evident through the Law of Attraction that states like attracts like.

It is important to endeavor to raise the vibration of our consciousness through meditation. Meditation is the way of finding out and becoming increasingly more aware of who we truly are. When we grow in consciousness, our lives start to reflect the qualities embedded in this higher state. We want to extend love, to be of service. We feel more trustful, hopeful, thankful, thereby attracting to us trustworthy people, positive incidents and situations, and many, many things for which to be grateful.

And when one person grows in consciousness, it contributes to raising the consciousness of others. In other words, we can say that consciousness is contagious.

We increase our capacity to love and everything that emanates from it as we continue to raise our consciousness to a more refined vibration. When we speak of "higher consciousness", it is not a state to be achieved, and that's it. The progressive levels of higher consciousness go on and on, continue into eternity. This means the caliber of our vibrational level of consciousness can continue to more refined intense states of love, joy, and peace.

ONLY THE THINKING MIND

You are not only the thinking mind, which is limited by what it perceives from your five external senses that can often be misleading. It knows only of the past and from that projects the future.

We need our thinking mind to study for tests, take instruction on how to use our computer, learn to paint, drive a car, practice our profession or craft be it an auto mechanic, carpenter, teacher, nurse, doctor, lawyer, scientist, to name several. Those who achieve excellence in their profession or craft and contribute to others at a high level of quality attest to the importance of consistently applied focused thinking in order to do so.

The thinking mind is also a required tool for accomplishing things in our daily lives. We need to plan our grocery list, our next doctor's appointment, our agenda for the next business meeting, our next holiday, although it may be still six months away.

Much of the time we are not in control of our thinking. The thinking mind seems to have a life of its own, and when not focused on a specific task, event or sequenced logic often creates thoughts, emotions, assumptions, judgments that arise seemingly unbidden. And while we can have positive thoughts, often they are negative and therefore unwelcome.

Most thoughts are also highly repetitive because they are conditioned. It has been estimated that of the 12-60 thousand thoughts we have a day, 95% of them are repetitive and of those thoughts, 80% are negative.[1] All repetitive thoughts are based on past experiences. Habitual thinking patterns incline us to think, perceive, approach, and interact with our environment and others in habitual ways. How many times have we witnessed ourselves behaving in the same non-productive or reactive ways? How many times have we heard ourselves or others repeat the same sayings or stories, regardless of their relevance to the current conversational context?

Our thoughts can torture us at times. They can create imagined fears, remind us of unfulfilled ambitions, evoke feelings of being less than or not good enough. They unearth regrets, guilt, envy, and anger as easily as a pitchfork unearths moist soft soil. The Buddha said, "Whatsoever an enemy might do to an enemy or a foe to a foe, the ill-directed mind can do to you and even worse." [2]

When the mind is not focused, if someone could record our thoughts and play them back to us, they would likely drive us crazy – repetitive, boring, nonsensical, absurd and often disturbing. Although heard internally, that's exactly what they do: drive us crazy, which further drives us to compulsive behaviors to distract ourselves from such thoughts.

Although, at times, it may seem to us that our thoughts come from "out of the blue", most of them come, in fact, from conditioned earlier patterns of thought. They can also enter from the collective human consciousness since we are all connected.

We now know of the neuroplasticity of our brains. Our brains are malleable. Conditioned thinking repeatedly follows the same neural network patterns, which establish "grooves" that can be very deep. This can lead to distractive thinking that is unrelated to what we are experiencing in the present. The good news is that because of the brain's malleability, we can retrain our brains to establish new and healthier neuro networks. We can influence our brain to think in more positive, productive ways.

An average person's mind wanders about 50% of their awaking hours. [3] Our thoughts flit and fly, but often more like disturbing bats than butterflies.

HOW do we find the "off switch" for this often spooky and disturbing compulsive thinking mind?

THE DIFFERENCE BETWEEN THINKING AND AWARENESS

One can get confused with the use of the terms "awareness" and "consciousness", as often they are used synonymously, and I do so at times in this book. However, in the following, I am using awareness as a particular from of consciousness that I describe.

Both thinking and awareness are different levels of consciousness. To have a thought is essentially different from being aware. All thoughts, including positive thoughts, as already mentioned, tend to be conditioned. There is a vast difference between thinking and awareness, the latter being of a much higher order of consciousness. Awareness comes from no thought and is usually accessed through inner stillness. And when awareness comes, it is experienced as fresh and new.

The thinking mind can't grasp awareness. On the whole, it is divisive. It only exists in activity as thought. It differentiates everything, reduces everything to one thought at a time, although it can link thoughts in a logical order and thereby reason deductively and inductively and remember. Awareness has a quality of spaciousness about it. It is free of grasping and allows all things to simply emerge. You don't have to try to hold on to awareness like a thought you want to remember, since once aware of something, always aware of it.

Awareness is devoid of any tension. Often when you are unhappy, it is the mind that is active and not directed on a specific thing or task so the thoughts you have can easily create uncomfortable emotions. Is this not true? It is the ill-directed mind that makes problems. Stop the runaway mind by going into stillness in the present moment. When you are alone or in nature, look around you and notice the stillness in what you see, including the space around everything. Do you find unease and conflict there? We will practice going into stillness later.

The thinking mind is part of consciousness but is a limited and from experience we know it can often be a disturbing aspect of it. If we can get it to lie down, so to speak, when it is not assisting us in an efficient way and become still, it is no longer an impediment to accessing awareness. When the mind is in focused or unfocused thought mode, it actually obstructs the natural flow of higher awareness. It behaves like a world onto itself instead of a tool to navigate everyday practical life and be of use in acquiring knowledge to further explore possibilities.

Awareness is much swifter than the thinking mind. Through awareness, you don't need to deliberate to know if something is true or false. You just "know".

The thinking mind is an instrument. We may liken it to a pencil. We use a pencil to write, add sums, draw, et cetera. When we have finished with it, we put it down. We don't identify with it. A car too is an instrument that helps us get from one place to another. Although some people falsely identify with their car as an extension of who they are, it is just a tool. When we identify with the instrument of the thinking mind as who we are, herein lies the danger. We lose perspective and can't see beyond the mind's boundaries. In such a state, ego can take possession of our identity, building barricades and passing judgment. We suffer in life, not so much because of other people or circumstances but because of our egoic thinking.

The thinking mind is not sensitive to the more refined energy of higher consciousness. It is the energy of the level of consciousness in a person's words that mainly counts and the positive or negative energy their words give off. It's not only what a person says, but the level of consciousness from which they speak that influences us. Many people know intuitively when someone is speaking the truth from a state of awareness. They can literally feel the vibrational difference between mind-based speech and shared awareness.

Philosopher Renee Descartes in the 17th Century (1596-1650) set out to prove the existence of man. His conclusion: "I think, therefore I am." He equated thinking with Being. What a fatal error! And humans believed and lived by that limited and false definition for hundreds of years. Many still do.

AN EPIPHANY: EVIDENCE OF BREAKING THROUGH TO A HIGHER AWARENESS

Most of us at some time in our life have had an epiphany, a time when the mind, heart, and soul came together to see something in a new or different way. These are moments of sudden revelation or realization. Such moments are never forgotten, and our epiphany changes us in some way.

Astronaut Edgar Mitchell, now deceased, was the second man in space. On his second trip (1971), travelling with two other astronauts, he had an epiphany. Returning to earth and looking at all the space around him while also feeling a profound silence and stillness, he came to the awareness that we and everything in the Universe are One. This so changed Mitchell that after he returned to earth and normal life, he started the Institute of Noetic Sciences for the purpose of studying consciousness. This Institute is still very active today.

The following is an excerpt of Deepak Chopra's epiphany from Elise Ballard's book *Epiphany*:

"In 1980 I was practicing medicine in Boston, Massachusetts. It is a habit of mine to take a walk after meditation. One day, at about ten o'clock in the morning, I was taking my morning walk in the Fenway Park area, pondering why some of my patients were healing and others weren't.

"Suddenly, it hit me: People have the power to heal themselves.

"I had been observing over my years of practice the rare patients that had done so, who had recovered from their illnesses, and it occurred to me at this moment that there was one common factor – they moved from a place of fear to a place of extreme joy and what I would call the intoxication of love. It hit me that they all had the same kind of shift in consciousness. You know, it sounds simplistic when I say it, but actually the shift is very profound and deep. For 40 years people have been studying the effects of stress. But nobody had actually studied the biology of joy or love. So it occurred to me that that's where we need to move." [4]

Troy Mutter of Victoria, Canada, shared with me an epiphany he had:

"Partly through imagery, which then led to a new felt awareness, I had a clear vision of how we are all so connected. The initial perceptual shift was from 'me' to 'us'.

"When I am in a room with others, I now realize it is not 'me' and 'them' but 'us'.

"I came to see that everything undertaken or done for just 'me' is out of alignment with 'us', with the whole, and therefore cannot bring 'me' fulfillment.

"The 'me' cannot take sole credit for anything. Any achievement experienced by the 'me' was helped by many seen and unseen forces of the 'us'. Nothing really belongs to or can be owned by just 'me', since all is received and comes out of the collective 'us'.

"What I may think of as mine – my money, my car, my business, even my love do not come from and therefore belong to just 'me'. Also, when we are acting out of ego, pain, greed, these thoughts, actions, and emotions have their origin in and measurably come out of the collective 'us' – not just the 'us' we experience in this life time through our parents, siblings, culture, societal norms and conditioning, but those of our ancestors and their ancestors.

"In a flash, I came to see: It's not *me*; it's *us*. It's not *mine*; it's *ours*. There is no *me* or *you*, but *we*."

THE EGO

WHAT IS IT?

At one time in our evolution, we were hunters and gatherers. We needed to fight to acquire our food, to defend our lives, and protect our loved ones and clan. The ego then served as a construct for protection and in this helpful role still does today, some examples being: when we are careful when crossing the street, take care of our health, remind ourselves to buckle up our car seatbelt, be vigilant about the safety of our children, or when we legitimately need to defend ourselves.

The ego is still part of the human condition but has now taken on a role that often works against our welfare, especially our emotional, psychic, and spiritual welfare. The dysfunctional ego has become a false self that believes it is separate from others and therefore needs to be on the defensive with others, constantly compare itself with others. It can inflate our self-concept in one minute and take us down in the next. For the inflated, dominating ego, this involves trying to be better than, richer than, more powerful than, more threatening than others. For the wounded egoic self, it means living mainly in fear, being a victim, feeling not good enough or able to overcome life's challenges.

The ego now pretends to be who we are, but if we find out it is not who we truly are, it will no longer be able to trick us into believing we are separate, needy, weak and so need to prove we are more than or not good enough when we compare ourselves to others. The ego pulls a veil down between who it tells us we are and the awareness of the truth of who we really are.

Its required partner is the thinking mind. If we have not tamed the ego - and predictably most of us have not - its influence on us can actually be seen as a kind of hypnotism, a mesmerizing influence.

The ego's strong and only tool to keep us under its influence, keep us in its control, and to keep itself alive is to evoke FEAR in all its obvious and subtle forms. Therefore, whenever we are coming from fear, we are coming from ego. When we are upset or don't feel our own inner worth, strength, or peace; when we feel a need to bully or dominate others, the ego is in control. If we look deeply enough, underlying such feelings or thoughts is fear. When we are not at peace, it is wise to ask ourselves, "Where is the fear in this?" This is a way of finding out the ego. Once we can recognize the ego in ourselves, we can break identification with it so it can no longer pretend to be us. The additional benefit is that we can then see beyond the ego in others and know also that it is not who they truly are.

We have all been heavily conditioned to believe we have to fear others, or at least some. Through the fear-evoking ego, we all share in anger, frustration, envy, insecurity, the need to control, and so on. This egoic conditioning comes from family, communities, religious upbringing, our educational systems, national culture, the ever-present and blasting media, and general worldwide human belief systems.

Before we come to know the truth of who we truly are, we are basing our "truth" on beliefs, theories, hearsay, prenatal and early childhood influences, the beliefs and sometimes superstitions of our parents and previous generations, on cultural mores, and multicultural generational beliefs. We are the recipients of these influences. We have not been living from our true Self.

I have often mused about where the ego came from, how it came into existence. Of course, there is the metaphorical biblical story of the Garden of Eden. Were Adam and Eve tempted to see themselves as separate and needing to fear for their survival in a moment of poor choice by believing they could somehow separate themselves from their Source? From an evolutionary view, did the ego endure and change beyond the need for humans to be hunters and gatherers and literally fight for survival? And if so, when? When humans evolved to have a sufficiently sized cranial frontal lobe that enabled self-reflective consciousness? This would have led to the ability to break from group mind to thinking as an individual self. And once thinking individually, one saw oneself as separate from others and in a fearful world of one's own.

HOW CAN WE RECOGNIZE THE EGO IN OUR LIVES?

In order to break from the dysfunctional ego, we need to recognize when it is operating in our lives. And for many, it is in operation most of our waking hours. As already stated, when we can recognize the ego in operation, we have already broken from our identification with it as who we are. The ego then starts to get weaker, have less of a hold on us. In response, it feels threatened and vulnerable so steps up its need to protect itself by trying myriad ways to indicate it is still in control. One way it can try to weaken us is by making us feel small. One person said after she made a significant mistake at work, she "felt so small she could sit on a dime and swing her legs." She equated her work mistake with who she was. Haven't we all felt such low self-worth at times? And doesn't that render us less confident we can do better next time?

We have all experienced the torturing ego in our lives. Even if something wonderful happens to us to make us feel like we have succeeded, won, achieved some goal, there is the lingering thought that we may lose what we have achieved or not make it when the next challenge comes around the corner.

It is evident that the ego uses the idle or worrying mind as its conduit to keep us under its control. Become aware of your thoughts. When is the ego speaking and not the real you?

Some of the many faces of the ego:

· FEAR – based on mental or emotional situations, not on real life-or-death situations or when you truly have to physically defend or take care of yourself or another;
· When motivated by self-interest or self-concern only;
· When your internal dialogue is negative, such as when judging, complaining, blaming;
· When making comparisons by feeling superior to others in some way or feeling inferior to others in some way;
· When needing to get your sense of worth or identity from others such as when "name dropping" of those you know who are famous, wealthy, have a high positive public profile, or are renowned for some achievement, thereby trying to build yourself up by association;
· When purposely withholding due credit or acknowledgment from someone or claiming their achievement as yours.
· When you are uncompromisingly opinionated, seek power over others, become defensive, seek perfectionism, feel self-righteous, are prideful, and so on.

The machinations and tricks the ego plays are endless. A few subtle ways the ego shows itself are through self-sabotage, gossiping, and attachments. We have to be like an alert Sherlock, at times, to find it out.

Although identification with the ego has brought with it suffering, to be "against" it or demonize it is not wise. Although problematic, at times, it is still part of our consciousness, and we don't want to reject any part of our Self. The ego has served a purpose in our evolution; however, the problematic ego has run its course. It is not helpful. Due to the pain and insanity we have experienced because of it, we now see the need for and are motivated to go beyond its painful impediments so as to come into awareness of our true Self.

PRACTICE
Take 10 minutes over each of 3 sequential days to notice your thoughts. Identify those when you are coming from the fear-evoking ego. When you identify them as coming from the ego, drop them. Say to yourself, "No way am I going to feed the ego."

OUR QUEST FOR AN IDENTITY

Because most of us are identified with the egoic self, at least to some degree, we don't feel "right" or complete a lot of the time. Something is still missing. Hence our feelings such as we just haven't made it yet, we need to do better next time, or that there must be more to life than this. The ego can use our lack of fulfillment to its benefit by having us seek an alternative in another false egoic self-image. For example, if we feel humiliated by being the poorest on the block when we were growing up, it can entice us to strive to be the richest adult in the city or country, and often at great cost to ourselves and others.

Of course, it is then taking us once again down a wrong road and in the wrong direction, thus further away from our true identity. It wants to keep us on an endless search for what we can never find by following its road map.

It's interesting to observe how many of us search for an identity through whatever we can grab onto: our sexual orientation, our level of education, net worth, kind of car we drive, neighborhood we live in, green hair, tattoos, sports hats that indicate the team we support and are identified with.

Of course your unique expression is important and things can be enjoyed for their quality, comfort, beauty, and utility. Abundance is wonderful and to be enjoyed as long as we don't feed the ego and thereby get a false sense of who we are because of it. One way we can determine this is if we feel pleased when we attract attention or "puffed up" because we live in an affluent neighborhood, have a post-graduate degree, own an expensive vehicle, or wear high-end designer clothes, as some examples.

We also can add to our personal identity by what we have accomplished, how fortunate or unfortunate our lives have been, what we own or don't own, those we are for or against. We put all of our experiences and life events together and create a narrative of who we are. Then we falsely identify with this limited personal story.

Another less obvious level of self-identification is when we live vicariously through the accomplishments of others, especially our children, spouses, and partners. Their victories are our victories, their failures our failures. On one level this can be seen as a subtle form of identity theft.

IS THERE A HOW TO RID OURSELVES OF THE PROBLEMATIC EGO?

One afternoon, a group of us were discussing this very topic. One woman surmised that the ego dies only 10 minutes after the body has been declared officially dead. Of course, we all laughed. But there is a seriousness here as well in that it points to how difficult it is to free ourselves from the grip of the ego.

First of all, we need to recognize if we have falsely identified with the ego as who we are. Next, we have to become mindful of when the ego is operating in ourselves. Another effective way is to not seek attention for anything from others. However, the most damaging thing we can do to the ego is to meditate regularly, since meditation is the way for us to become more and more of who we truly are in all our magnificence. As we continue to meditate, the ego will naturally begin to lose its power, its hold on us and begin to diminish. It cannot survive for long in the awareness we find in inner stillness that we experience through a number of means, but especially meditation. When we come from an awareness of our true Self, there is no longer any room for fear.

In addition, when we meditate, we are in the present moment. The ego, because it is so intertwined with the thinking mind, lives in the past and the future and tries to draw us into them. When we are in the past, often we are feeling regret and are not accessing the gifts of the present moment. And it is by coming from our past that we bring our conditioning forward. If you want to put the ego in a corner, so to speak, whenever you find yourself in the past or future, bring yourself back to what is happening in your experience now. Then see if you can find the ego.

There is a variation on a famous Zen story that illustrates this beautifully:

One day, two monks were out horseback riding. One was an elder and the other a novice. In time, they came to a river. On the other side was a woman in distress. She didn't know if she could make it across, and even if she did, she would ruin her new dress. When she saw the monks appear, she asked if they could please help her cross over the river. Without hesitation the elder monk crossed over the river, picked the lady up and put her behind him on his horse. When she was safely on the other side, he helped her down. After she expressed her gratitude, she went on her way.

The monks then continued to ride on. About an hour later, the novice monk said, "You have done something terribly wrong. Our Order requires us to not touch a woman."

The elder monk replied, "I left that woman back at the river. You are still carrying her."

4

THE HOW OF NOW

GATEWAYS INTO THE PRESENT MOMENT

There was a fellow who attended a major 3-day workshop in Vancouver, Canada, where the teacher helps the participants look at their past, determine the burdens they are still carrying from it, and facilitates their letting go of these impediments to their happiness. It is quite cathartic.

After the workshop was over, this fellow went up to the teacher and said, "I just don't know how to let go of a major hurt."

The teacher replied, "Just be here Now." The student continued, "But I don't know HOW to be here Now."

The teacher reiterated, "Just be here Now."

The student could only respond again, "But I don't know HOW."

Many of us talk about the importance of living in the Now – the only real, powerful, and creative instant of our life, yet what does that mean? We can utter the words, "I am here now", look around us and notice what and who is in front of us, yet still not come from the animating presence we experience when truly in the Now.

Credit and gratitude must be given to spiritual teacher Eckhart Tolle for helping us come into the felt *experience* of the Now. He presented to us 5 portals or gateways into the experience of the present moment.

THE BREATH

On average a person takes 2,300 breaths a day. Yet how many of us stop even a couple of times a day to take a conscious breath? To take a conscious breath means simply to become aware of your breath, to notice it. Breathing is required for human life and it is also an avenue to the spiritual life. Our autonomic nervous system operates without any effort on our part. It includes such things as our digestive, pulmonary, and respiratory systems.

Although our breathing is automatic, at this time in human evolution, it is the one part of the autonomic bodily systems that we have some conscious control over. For example, we can choose to lengthen or shorten our in breath and out breath and extend the time we hold the breath after intake. There are many different forms of breathing we have control over, all which can fall under the category "Breath Work". Each form of breath work has a specific purpose and benefit, many of which are to help us release past pain still held in the body and also to bring us into a state of inner calm and stillness.

PRACTICE

When you have the time to be quiet and sit alone for 10 minutes, observe your breath. Just gently notice it. In doing so, you are taking attention away from the compulsive thinking mind while noticing the life force in your body. This in itself is an excellent meditation. Do it as often and as long as you are prompted to do so.

In terms of the above practice, you may come to notice the out breath being longer than the in breath and that at the point of your nostrils when you take in a breath, the air is cooler than when you exhale. You may become aware of your torso rising and falling with each complete inhale and exhale. You may notice that as you watch your breath, you started to feel calmer, more relaxed. As you continue in this practice you may also notice the out breath getting even longer; additionally, you may notice that at the end of the out breath, there is a pause of stillness.

When you come from the witness position, you are watching, not thinking or judging and therefore coming from a higher state of consciousness. If in doing the above practice you notice that there is, indeed, a pause of stillness after the out breath and before the in breath – the longer you continue in this meditative practice, the longer the pause usually gets. How wonderful! We have stillness built right into the process of our breathing, our very source of physical life. Stillness is not just an aspect of who we truly are: stillness enables us to access all the aspects of our Being. As such, we could look upon stillness as the bedrock of our true Self.

SILENCE

Ahh, silence. What a rare thing to experience in our modern world, especially in urban settings. We are bombarded by noise: the roar of traffic, the noise of numerous machines, the varied noises that fill our malls, restaurants that blare out loud music that, combined with the chatter of those at tables nearby, can make it difficult to even hear our companion across the table, the noise of construction, the roar of jet planes overhead, the numerous and loud noises that fill our airports, the often heightened volume and frenetic tone of what we watch on TV, especially the news and commercials. In addition to living with all this outer noise, we have the noisy thinking mind to contend with.

Where can we go to find silence? Walks in nature, keeping our own homes quiet, stepping into our quiet meditation space and going inward. The space within us is noiseless. When we are aware enough to notice the silence around and in us, we are in the present moment. And we find ourselves alert. Silence is also a segue into inner stillness.

STILLNESS

How do we know when we are in a state of inner stillness? Inner stillness means *no thought*. It is a *felt* state. Inner stillness is not static or boring. It is extremely active, full of the energy frequency of higher consciousness. An apt analogy is of a fan when we start it up. First the blades go slowly, then speed up, going increasingly faster until we see just a still round disk.

THE INNER BODY

The inner body? What is that? I am not referring to our lungs, knees, kidneys and so forth but the animating life force within us that is consciousness itself. We are conscious beings. However, I know of only a few spiritual teachers like Eckhart Tolle and Barry Long who have brought our attention to the inner body, its import, and how to activate consciousness through Inner Body Meditation. When you are feeling your inner body, attention is taken away from the thinking mind.

ACCEPTANCE

When we do not resist life, when we fully accept our experiences and others just as they are, we are in the present moment. Full attention to something without judging is acceptance as well. When we fully accept our life and others just as they are, we have no resistance to them. Then, life can flow more easily, effortless, and joyfully through us.

In addition, when we experience joy, sincere gratitude, heartfelt appreciation, laughter, and peace, we know we are in the present moment.

5

DIVING DEEPER INTO STILLNESS

THE EXPERIENCE OF STILLNESS

The shift in consciousness we need requires that we discover and live from the stillness within us. When we come from inner stillness, which, as already stated, is paradoxically a highly active, alert state, it opens us to experience aspects of our true Self and continues to pave the way to felt Self-realization.

Noise is the language of the world and to quote Rumi, "Silence is the language God speaks, all else is a poor translation." Silence, however beautifully caressing, is not stillness. Stillness is a deep inner state. As mentioned earlier, when we are aware of silence, we are in the present moment, and silence is also an invitation to enter into stillness, especially during the early stages of practicing meditation.

To sit in stillness is to allow everything to be as it is. Exclude nothing from your awareness. This includes the whirring of the fan, the ticking of the clock, the noise of the traffic outside, the "ding" from your mobile phone signaling you have a new message. It also includes any thoughts that come to you or emotions that arise. If you try to exclude anything from stillness, you are in resistance. It's impossible to be still and to be in resistance at the same time.

While you are abiding in inner stillness, you are aware of and accept everything that is taking place on the inner plane as well as in the outer world around you. Your intent is to become so anchored in stillness that you approach everything you do from this state of stillness, regardless of where you are or who you are with. It is in stillness that the greatest authentic power is released. I often refer to stillness as, for some, the newly discovered and only authentic "Super Power". That which cannot be mentally grasped, only experienced, is at work nourishing your soul and therefore positively influencing all of your thoughts, words, and actions.

It has been said, "Be still and know that I am God." [1] We find God in the stillness within us. Many equate God as being the essence of love. Aren't we all searching for love? But aren't most of us searching for it from others outside of ourselves. If we change our understanding of this quote to mean within stillness we will know that we are love, then why don't we try to find the love that we already are by entering the stillness within us?

Because we feel so "at home" and complete in a state of stillness, the more often we enter inner stillness, the less likely we will want to be in noisy environments and surrounded by people who chatter of mundane, superficial things and often in an agitated manner. We may not listen to the car radio as much and our interest in watching TV may decline. We will likely become more comfortable with non-verbal yet deep communication in our relationships, since we are now able to relate to others from a deeper place than surface thoughts and emotions. We will also experience an increasing delight in just sitting with ourselves in stillness. Indeed, we will find that in stillness we feel least alone because then we are in touch with our One Self.

It is in stillness that we can hear the inner voice of our higher awareness that speaks to us in "words" without sound or form, of things we cannot become aware of in any other way.

When we enter into stillness, we cultivate an alert attention. As we listen to the stillness by putting attention on our ears, especially our inner ear canals, it creates a kind of vacuum, so to speak, into which we invite the wisdom of higher consciousness. And as we continue in the practice of listening to the "still small voice" within us, it increasingly guides our thoughts, perceptions, actions, and words, until there comes a time when if we need to know or do something, we automatically go inward and listen. When we pray, we often use words to make requests. When we listen in stillness, we receive what the consciousness within us wants to share with us, wants us to become aware of.

TAKE VISION INTO STILLNESS

It isn't the wealthy, the powerful, the famous who are going to solve our planet's problems. Not even education, helpful though it is, will bring us the global solutions that are needed today. Pursuing these paths has only served to highlight the inability of our minds and actions to move beyond our differences. It is time for us to recognize that *stillness is the way*.

Inner stillness is refined consciousness; therefore, it is highly causative, highly creative. All fresh and new ideas come out of the womb of inner stillness, since in stillness we are able to tap into universal consciousness. This is vastly more reliable than the solutions that come from the limited, conditioned thinking mind that almost always bases its solutions on what was relevant in the past, not on what is most appropriate for the present situation and which is the best way we can also prepare for the unpredictable emerging future.

When stillness is our foundation, we don't hungrily look outside of ourselves for answers but rather allow for insights and solutions to emerge naturally from within us. We allow the wisdom within us to correct our perceptions and to guide our thoughts, dialogues, and efforts until positive solutions come. We come to understand through experience that everything we need or need to know is already within us. Does a man who owns a 500-acre apple orchard run up and down the highway begging for apples?

How do we still the mind? By placing our attention on the present moment. Just bringing attention to our breath until we feel a state of calmness can help us do this. If we notice that we have drifted away from the present moment, then we bring our attention gently back to the breath again.

A still mind is unfamiliar to many, if not most of us, so we have to learn HOW to experience such a state.

It is important not to make an effort in order to bring our attention into the present moment. A still mind is not a forced mind. It is a mind at ease. Any effort to stay in the Now comes from thinking about what we need to do, and thinking is not stillness. It is also important not to make any judgment about how effective we are in holding to the present moment, because all such assessment also involves thinking. We cannot break free from mental chatter by using our mind.

When you begin the practice of sitting in stillness, simply pay attention to what you are experiencing at that time and begin to take some conscious breaths. This is the opposite of concentration. Concentration is an exercise of thought. It requires a tight mental focus. You cannot enter stillness by concentrating. Paying attention to the present moment is more of a full body experience. There is a fullness about it. All you need do is rest in the present moment and what the present moment contains. Feel what it feels like to be in your body. Witness your breathing. Be open to all of your senses – both outer and inner.

When you are inwardly still, you get in touch with your own essence. How good it feels to be who you truly are! As already mentioned, once you are in touch with the life within, you come to realize this same life force is within everybody. We all share in the same animating Presence. As you continue to spend time in stillness, cultivating awareness of your inner Presence, you begin to *feel* that same Presence, that aliveness in the people and world around you.

This purposeful entering into stillness was demonstrated by the Master Jesus. As the biblical story goes, the town folk caught a woman in the act of adultery and brought her to him to ask if they were not right in stoning her to death for breaking the law. The woman's accusers were certain they had Jesus cornered. Was he going to openly advocate breaking the law?

Jesus was on the spot. In that critical moment, how did he respond? Instead of answering right away, he entered into stillness. Bending down, he began writing in the sand. We have no evidence of what he wrote or even that he wrote anything meaningful. I see his writing in the sand as a delay tactic. The townsfolk wanted Jesus' response immediately, yet Jesus knew that he had to first go into stillness to access his answer. What came forth from those few moments of stillness are some of the most powerful words ever spoken: "He that is without sin among you, let him first cast a stone at her." ² Presented with this challenge, the townsfolk themselves were now on the spot. One by one they slunk away, leaving the woman standing alone with Jesus.

 The consciousness in stillness is the field of infinite potentiality out of which we create from our inner reality our personal experiences and our outer world. All fresh answers come out of stillness. It is through stillness that all perplexing issues are solvable. When we live our lives from the inside out, we are alerted to all we need to know by our "Inner Knower". We stop seeking fulfillment outside ourselves, and we enjoy an inner contentment and confidence in living. The external fear-evoking world loses its hold on us.

STILLNESS IN THE CORRIDORS OF POWER?

When on a chartered bus trip through Ireland, I listened to three women engaged in conversation in response to a news article they had read that morning about global violence. "I don't see why such violence has to continue," said one of the women. "I don't see why we can't just all live in peace."

The other two women immediately reacted: "Oh, come on. You are talking Pollyanna. We are never going to change the way the world is. It's always been like this."

The world has changed and will continue to change. Indeed, it must. If you are reading this now, you surely must feel there is a way to reduce personal suffering and to achieve inner and world peace.

When people come together and sit in stillness or meditate together, surface differences normally dissolve. There are no judgments – only a shared experience of a bonding of acceptance and unity.

Let's envision the day coming, and coming soon, when the world's leaders sit together in stillness prior to and periodically during their deliberations. When their course of action remains unclear, there will be no haggling or jockeying for national advantage, no cajoling, haranguing, or threatening. They will know it is time for a different kind of "ceasefire" and enter stillness out of which will eventually come a better way for all concerned. Just like the two women on the bus, some of us may see this as an impossible dream.

However, it is important to believe this new way of being in the world is possible and with that belief and commitment to acting on it will come the energy, knowing, and creativity to make it so.

Imagine that in the near future stillness will be recognized as the way to solve differences in relationships as well as tackle our planet's problems. Envision a day when couples and families will regularly take time out to sit in stillness together before having dinner or entering some activity or serious conversation; when corporations, institutions, and governments, seeing the value of stillness, happily sanction "stillness breaks". Imagine a workplace in which people are truly present with each other.

Let's anticipate whenever creative solutions are required so that the needs of all or as many as possible are met, leaders will take the time needed to replenish their souls. By entering into stillness, they will be able to leave their habitual thinking patterns behind, thereby creating "inner" space for changed perceptions and new awareness to emerge to guide them. Going into stillness is almost always followed by a creative phase. Out of this "time out", novel solutions to longstanding problems can arise. By entering into stillness and invoking a deep spiritual wisdom, the leaders of the future will more readily *know* the noble course of action to take.

OUR NEED FOR A NOBLE VISION

Admittedly, this is a visionary book, but necessarily so, for "Where there is no vision, the people perish."[3]

It is up to each of us to create a vision for our personal world, then live our lives in such a way that we start closing the gap between what we are currently experiencing that falls short of our vision of what we would like to see.

When you are engaged in something or are drawn into a situation or argument, ask yourself the question: "What does this have to do with my personal vision?" The causative level of everything is within. You can be so tempted to address external issues and believe that by fiddling with effects, you are making changes. But nothing really changes unless the change is initiated from your inner Being.

Causes we become involved in need to flow from our inner state concurrently with our deepening consciousness. There are many noble causes. However, if we are not attentive, we can let ourselves get drawn into all sorts of diversions. This requires a focus on and ongoing attention to our vision.

Also, do dream globally. *Imagine* the time when the leaders of nations function not from ambition but from their common responsibility to be servant leaders for all humanity. *Imagine* what could emerge if, instead of posturing to save face before their publics, the emissaries of nations set aside issues of national and personal ego and sought solutions that would benefit all concerned. *Imagine* if collectively, world leaders entered into stillness and from there sought answers to the world's troubles. *Imagine* that soon there will be a level of international leadership that would articulate a noble global vision for all humanity based on human dignity and worth of all, and then call on each and every country and every one of us to move together toward achieving this vision.

Imagine a world in which we deal with each other from a sense of our Oneness as a species. Dream of each and every one of us accepting the responsibility of being custodians of each other and of our planet.

AUTHENTIC LEADERSHIP

Let us hold to the faith that more leaders will emerge who are well acquainted with the practice of stillness and likely engage in other spiritual practices as well. Why? Because an authentic leader is true to their own Being, which is spiritual. Because they have mainly gone beyond the restrictions of the ego, they will be authentic, honestly admitting their imperfections. They will exude a confidence that comes with Self-awareness. Because of their practice of mindfulness, they will exhibit behaviors that many will admire in them. In addition, because out of stillness comes creativity, they will be highly creative, innovative, and easily think "outside of the box", thereby pointing the way to new solutions to our current and emerging challenges.

PRACTICE
Consider then write down your personal vision for your life. Then hold to that vision. If it changes over time, acknowledge that and write it anew. Then, hold to that.

PRACTICE
Consider then write down your personal vision for all humanity. Then hold to that vision. If it changes over time, acknowledge that and write it anew. Then, hold to that.

6

AN EXPLORATION INTO ACCEPTANCE

The ego will see acceptance as giving in and surrender as admitting defeat.

As we know, one of the portals into the Now is full acceptance of what we are experiencing in the moment. It's easy to accept things when all is going well, but more difficult, of course, when situations are challenging us, evoking states of fear, anxiety, grief, sadness, or upset over change of any kind.

Our natural tendency is to go into resistance of what is during such challenging times and not be open to full acceptance. That's why it is important to practice acceptance at all times, happy, neutral, or painful so when challenging things happen and when resistance wants to win the day, we can stay in a state of trust and acceptance.

Acceptance opens us to the reality of what is. We are calm, clear minded, not controlled by our emotions. In this state, we know whether or not to take action, and if to take action, what the best course will be.

Resistance brings with it the energy charge of "against" and on one level can be seen as anti-life. If we truly lived with the awareness that Life is for us, even when it appears not to be, that it is always prompting us to grow in awareness of our true Self or to come from our true Self, we would find it easier to move into acceptance.

When we find that we can't accept something, then let's try to just *let it be*. In that way we are avoiding resistance, a cause of emotional and psychological pain. Unless it is a matter of self-defense, if we are against someone, a group, leader, or institution, we are coming from either or both self-interest and a sense of vulnerability. This is not to say that our position is not correct for us at the time; however, we can never see the whole of the situation and how it fits into the larger whole of our life or the evolution of human life itself. If we think we can, we are, figuratively speaking, purblind.

"But how can I in any way accept such things as genocide, violent rape, human trafficking and other heinous acts? Some things are just not to be accepted, tolerated."

I agree. Acceptance doesn't mean ignoring what happened and trying to deny or forget it. In situations like these, you can only accept that these terrible things happened and continue to happen in our world, but that does not mean that you condone them in any measure. You speak out against such inhumane acts. You call them out for what they are: destructive and often criminal acts that must be stopped, and you take whatever action you can to bring such unconsciousness to an end. You speak up because justice cries out to be done in such situations, but every effort should be made to respond to injustice in a rehabilitative way — a way that does not cause or provoke further inhumane actions. To react with fear or fear disguised as anger will not transform such hurtful acts. In addition, we, in contrast, can choose to continue to live our lives in a way that we are responsible for how our actions affect others.

Another less obvious form of acceptance is to admit you don't know about something. You don't know if something is, on balance, more positive or negative; you don't know if one political party is better than another to lead your country at a particular time; you don't know if that person consciously betrayed you or not. When you admit you don't know, you are not in resistance, pressing for an answer or feeling you have to take a position. You just rest in the unknowing and let things be as they are while waiting to see if clarity comes.

"Is there a HOW to make it easier to accept what life brings?"

Yes. This requires a change of your mind or your perception.

When we realize that as extensions of Source, our true Self can never be threatened, this assurance will enable us to move more easily into acceptance even under the most trying times. In addition, let us see if we can change our perception from life happens to us *to* life happens *for* us. If we can, we will receive everything with thanksgiving. Life is wanting to wake us up to a higher level of consciousness, and we are here on earth now challenged to do just that. This is our common human purpose.

Resistance causes a tightening within our body and mind. We contract and are not then open to the flow of the healing and corrective intelligence of Life itself. Just say to yourself, "I am for" something or someone, then follow it with "I am against" someone or something and notice how you feel the difference viscerally in your body. To "be for" opens you to Life. To "be against" closes you to it. That's why empowering visionaries who are for a noble cause attract like-spirited people and effect positive change. If you come from a position of being "against", you are not likely to achieve your goal, or if you do, the achievement will predictably not last long, since it is difficult to sustain something that comes out of the negative energy of "against". This, of course, does not mean that you do not stand up for your principles or rights.

"Is acceptance different from surrender? Is surrender a deeper, a more challenging form of acceptance? Is surrender more like a letting go? Does it even involve letting go of the question "Why"?

Only through your felt experience can you determine this for yourself with regards to a situation.

How can we just accept the diagnosis of a terminal illness, the loss of a child, a near fatal injury that leaves us incapacitated, the collapse of what formerly were healthy family dynamics?

When such deeply painful things happen to ourselves, our loved ones, or others, and we can do nothing about them, we are then forced into acceptance. If we do so grudgingly, this is not true acceptance. Willing and full surrender in such painful circumstances is deeply challenging, but also usually brings with it an intense spiritual transformative and healing power. Sometimes when a person completely surrenders, it is through an act of grace, and after their total surrender, they experience an ongoing joy and excitement in living.

Yes, we have to accept what has happened, because it happened, but it can take a long time to surrender to what it leaves in its wake. Deep and full surrender to such as the loss of a loved one or the life-threatening addiction of a child normally happens over a period of time. In most instances, when one thinks they have surrendered, it later becomes obvious they haven't fully. The stages of surrendering can seem endless, like those of grieving. We cry out, "Oh, when will I know when I have fully surrendered?" A wise spiritual teacher ended his book, *The Power of Now* by answering, "When you no longer need to ask the question."

And what about forgiveness, of surrendering to some deep pain caused by another person? We can say we have accepted what has hurt us and forgiven the person; however, have we really? Complete forgiveness may take a long time too. When we no longer hold any pain or even remember what we need to forgive, our forgiveness is total, and what a blessing that is to ourselves and the other person. Another indication that we have forgiven our "enemy" is that we pray for them, for their welfare.

Acceptance can also be seen as peaceful resistance. Being peaceful, we do not come from an intent of doing harm or subjugating others. This was so beautifully illustrated on the world scene by Mahatma Gandhi and Martin Luther King. Just as there is amazing power in acceptance and surrender, so too there is in peaceful resistance. Peaceful resistance is not *against* a perceived injustice, it is *for* justice. What is the nature of this power? Knowing we are standing up for justice and a better world. Knowing that we are coming from love for our community, however large it may be, or all of humanity.

When we come from peaceful resistance, we give no reason, no excuse to those we are standing up to to retaliate in an aggressive way.

Let us read, then pause and take in the following words of Martin Luther King.

"Power properly understood is nothing but the ability to achieve purpose. And one of the great problems of history is that the concepts of love and power have usually been contrasted as opposites, polar opposites, so that love is identified with resignation of power, and power with a denial of love. ...What is needed is a realization that power without love is reckless and abusive, and love without power is sentimental and anemic. Power at its best is love implementing the demands of justice, and justice at its best is love correcting everything that stands against love." [1]

When we look at the likes of heinous acts, on-going conflicts, deliberate subjugation, torture, which we personally cannot take specific action on because they are occurring in faraway places, how best can we respond? Do we simply accept this as the human condition at this time in our evolution? To avoid caring about things we feel we can do nothing about is to weaken only ourselves by cutting ourselves off from our brothers and sisters. To add our anger, judgment, accusations in such situations to the offending parties is futile. We are not helpless, however. If we have the financial means, we can contribute to organizations such as: Amnesty International, Oxfam, Doctors Without Borders, UNICEF, World Vision, and many more. We can hold to the intention of the highest good for all involved; we can say a prayer of loving kindness and send it to all humanity or a specific group in need. We can "cultivate our own garden", our own personal circumscribed world, by acting from love in all we do and all with whom we come in contact. This will ripple out to larger communities.

"When we come up against people who are uncaring and even aggressively want to hurt others, how can we accept their behavior?"

We don't accept it. We do what we can to stop their hurtful behaviors. Then, we hold compassion toward them, since they are still unconscious, meaning they are not yet at a level of caring for others or feeling responsible for their deleterious actions against others. Forgive such people. They are blinded by their solely self-centered ego so cannot stop their compulsive need to conquer others, have control over them, to get back at them through various means. They still have so many lessons ahead of them to learn in order to grow in consciousness in this schoolhouse called "Earth". Those with a mental or emotional imbalance likely do not understand why they lash out at others.

Most truly do not know why they are driven to harm others. Our ultimate challenge? They need our compassion, not rejection or punishment. Each of us is on our own trajectory, some further ahead than others on the path to a consciousness of caring for others; however, no matter how long it takes, all will eventually end up in the same destination of coming into our true Self.

7

MEDITATION AND MINDFULNESS

The Buddha was asked, "What have you gained from meditation?"
He replied, "Nothing. However, let me tell you what I have lost:
anger, anxiety, depression, insecurity, fear of death."

J. Krishnamurti

Some rare individuals have awakened to their true identity spontaneously, but often after experiencing severe suffering, others through devout prayer and service. Meditation, which leads one into a state of stillness, is perhaps the best way for most humans to find out who they truly are. Spiritual reading, spiritual practices, and also being in a spiritual community will accelerate this process. The longer you meditate regularly, the more you *experience* the true Self in you emerging. The layers of the false egoic-self start to fall away, so you increasingly become more aware of your true nature and your capacities. Through meditation, we can touch something within us that is eternal. And once we have *experienced* the eternal within us, we can no longer doubt that we are eternal.

THE MAN AND THE LOST KEY

There is a man out in the street in front of his home under a lamp post. He is searching with high agitation for something. He continues in this manner for some time.

A passerby stops and asks him, "What are you so eagerly looking for?"

The man responds, "The key to my house."

The passerby asks, "Did you lose it out here?"

"No, I left it in the house."

"Then why are you looking for it out here?" he asks.

"Because it is dark in the house." The man replies.

"Well, why don't you go inside and turn on the light?"

"Oh, great idea!" The man then went into his home, turned on the light and found the key right there on the table.

Many of us are like the man looking for the key to his home outside, where he cannot find it.

"Home" archetypally and symbolically usually represents one's life. Like the man, we won't be able to find the key to who we truly are unless we go inside our body and turn on the light of higher consciousness.

Almost all of humanity is still transfixed by the outside world – the world of material things, of mind concepts and sense experiences. Indeed, most of us are still "lost" in the external world.

"How can we avoid being 'lost in the world' if we have to work, shop, care for our families, pay bills, keep informed through the media, visit the doctor regularly, and so forth?"

Let us explore if we can be both in the world yet free of our attachments to it.

Just as when we are asked to identify what is around us, almost all will mention the objects: people, furniture, flowers, and so forth, but fail to notice the space that surrounds everything, which is usually more pervasive than the objects, most of us are not aware of the treasures we hold within the body. We have been told many times to look within. "The Kingdom is within." [1]

Are we like the man who lost the key to his house and needs someone to point out HOW to find it?

MEDITATION IS THE WAY –
THE WAY FROM CONFLICT TO PEACE

Through the powerful act of meditation, people come to realize the stillness within that is eternal and all-encompassing. This state of stillness is not personal but universal to all humanity – a fundamental shared element, which sadly for many is yet to be experienced, other than sporadically.

Up until now in human history, most have felt their separation from others, which has led to interpersonal discord and conflict in the world in myriad ways. However, the good news is that as human beings we instinctively also want to be connected to others, to gather with others, feel caring and empathy for and from others. This is an aspect of the push-pull of being human.

Meditation is a way to experience our Oneness. When a sufficient number of us realize our Oneness, it will reach a critical mass, a tipping point that can have an unstoppable and significant positive effect on humanity. It is through meditation we come to realize that not only am I my brothers' and sisters' keeper but I *am* my brothers and sisters.

"What about the other part of humanity that does not come to this realization and still wants to have control over or harm others either overtly or through deprivation?"

That is why our species needs to experience inner stillness by enough humans to bring about the tipping point to a higher consciousness for all.

"But what if this never occurs?"

Higher consciousness once achieved by individuals, even if not reaching the tipping point in our lifetime, will inform, will be the strongest influence in what humanity experiences hereafter. There is never a loss by moving to a higher state of consciousness.

Our world is not going to be saved solely by human systems, institutions, and high human intelligence, but more importantly by individuals who find and share the love that they are by going inward through meditation. If meditation is practiced on a worldwide scale, people will come to understand the loving and transformative power it is. This, of course, can only be realized by practicing it. And then, through our experience, we will make this a priority in our lives.

People spend years getting degrees, climbing the career ladder, acquiring things, worrying about their family, trying to improve their health, yet how often do they take time to try to understand *why* they experience what they do in their lives?

BENEFITS OF MEDITATION

There are many forms of meditation. All are valuable since they draw us into the present moment and take us inward. The benefits are myriad: from lowering our blood pressure and helping us sleep better to strengthening our immune system and preventing premature aging. All you have to do is search "meditation" on the internet and you will find pages and pages of the benefits of meditation, most of which are backed by hard science.

What are usually referred to as benefits of meditation can also be seen as outcomes. If you already meditate, a germane question to ask yourself is, "Why do I meditate?" Are your reasons outcomes of meditation, while meditation is the cause? If you don't limit your desired outcomes of practicing meditation, you open yourself to experiencing many more.

WHEN YOU MEDITATE, YOU DO NOT MEDITATE ONLY FOR YOURSELF

Our consciousness affects everyone around us. If a person meditates, they will affect others around them in a positive way. For example, if one person in a household meditates, it benefits all in that household. The same is true of communities such as church congregations, towns, and cities.

In 1976, this was documented by scientific research when the outcome of 1% of the a community that practiced Transcendental Meditation had the effect of bringing the crime rate down in that community by 16% on average.[2] Although there is yet little scientific evidence of the benefits of meditation to society as a collective, the myriad benefits to the person who meditates, including reduction of stress, anxiety, and depression, predictably point to outcomes such as a positive reduction in car accidents, suicides, mental illness and drug abuse.

Maharishi Mahesh, an Indian yogi brought to the attention of the world by the Beatles who learned Transcendental Meditation from him in his ashram in India, predicted that only 1% of the population meditating and coming from loving intentions would be sufficient to improve humanity's quality of life and usher in world peace.[3] If this is the case, given that there are approximately 7.8 billion people in our world currently, if one percent meditated regularly, meaning 78 million, we would see a different world. Individuals to groups to groups within groups meditating worldwide would bring more peace and harmony to humanity that would emanate from such meditations.

There are expressed differences of the required percentage to bring about such a global shift. The Rensselaer Polytechnic Institute in upper New York state, for example, conducted a scientific study in this area that indicated it would take 10% of the world population to hold to an unshakeable belief in world peace to bring it about. [4]

BENEFITS OF MEDITATING IN A GROUP

There are many benefits of meditating in a group. One of them is it provides an opportunity to raise our individual consciousness more quickly. The consciousness of the one in the group who is at that time at the highest level, by their very presence, will draw the others in the group toward that level. To use a metaphor, if there is a roaring fire, the kindling wood next to it will catch fire quickly.

When individuals join together in meditation, there is a compounded, a synergistic effect for all. And many people who meditate in a group attest to their being able to go deeper in their meditation when sitting together.

In deep meditation within a group, one can sometimes experience the felt melding of oneself and the individuals in the group into a sense of one field of Presence. What a beautiful way to experience our Oneness.

Being part of a caring community is healing. We derive strength from the acceptance and support we receive. We are allowed to be authentic and vulnerable without being judged. In our current times, when many families are spread out over the world, and if we engage many hours a day only with what is on the screen in front of us, it will be more challenging to find and build our communities.

Therefore, many will have to intentionally work to build and maintain family and community strength.

MEDITATION AND MINDFULNESS

More and more these days, we are hearing people talk of mindfulness and meditation. Sometimes they are used alone in a context and at other times synonymously or interchangeably.

Mindfulness is a particular type of awareness. As far as we know, the term wasn't specifically introduced until roughly 2,500 years ago by the Buddha.

Mindfulness means:
- Present moment-by-moment awareness of our experience as it unfolds.
- Mental alertness without the overlay of assumptions, judgments, evaluations, likes or dislikes, and conceptualizations.

In short, Mindfulness refers to the ability to give full, non-judgmental attention to our immediate experiences.

There is an analogy I have read that is appropriate here. Imagine your thinking mind in its predominant state is like a bottle of sandy water that has been shaken up. The particles in the water are all of your mostly erratic, disconnected thoughts that are swirling about in the water. When in this state, it is not easy to think clearly or even beyond your own immediate and pressing needs. However, if you simply put the jar down to rest on a table, the particles of sand will settle and the water will become clear. When the mind is calmed through meditation, it will naturally settle down and become clear, quiet, and serene.

To be able to live a mindful life, the practice of meditation is almost requisite. Meditation, through various processes, exercises, and practices helps us discipline the mind, bringing it to stillness and therefore to a state of clarity.

There are many forms of meditation most of which have the aim of bringing us into a state of mindfulness that, by dropping judgmental thinking, makes us open to accessing higher levels of consciousness and receiving new insights.

Mindfulness requires that we drop our past conditioning and egoic needs so we can see a person or situation in a clear way, without the screen of past experience, assumptions, and programming.

In addition, when we are mindful, we are more likely to become keen observers of ourselves — of how our mind works, what our thinking inclinations are. We can more easily witness ourselves and identify our biases, fears, and so on. This is why with committed regular practice, mindfulness can make us more aware of our immediate and direct experiences because when mindful, we are less captive of our conditioned and involuntary compulsive thinking and the emotions they evoke.

When mindful, our mind is still and alert, which is a precondition for deeper awareness and insight. Although we cannot force these states, through meditation that leads to mindfulness, we can clear the way for them to arise.

MISERABLE OR MINDFUL?

When my children were young and Christmas time came around, I made a very special effort one year to buy them unique and thoughtful gifts for their Christmas stockings. I took a long time picking out these presents and wrapped each of them carefully and in different paper.

Two days before Christmas Eve, I discovered they had gotten into their stockings, opened all the presents and re-wrapped them. I was furious. I called them and told them about all the work I did in making their stocking gifts very special this year and they ruined things by opening them before Christmas. I shouted at them to go up to their bedrooms immediately. The festive atmosphere in the house went down several notches.

If I had been mindful at the time, I would not have "lost it", got upset and yelled at my children but would have simply told myself, "My children are just being children. They were so anxious about Christmas and to find out what some of their presents were that they couldn't help themselves but open their stocking gifts."

A boy begged his father to help him make the basketball team at school by arranging for a basketball coach for him. The father spent hours to find a suitable basketball coach for his son and paid in advance for 3 lessons. Once he had accomplished this, he called his son and excitedly told him the good news to which the son replied, "Dad, I don't think I want to try out for the basketball team after all. The father was infuriated. He yelled at his son. "What? I went to all that trouble and expense to help you out because you asked me to and now you have decided you no longer want to keep playing basketball! You are such an unappreciative son." He slammed the phone down. That evening there was no talk around the dinner table, only the unspoken critical glare from the father to his son. When the father became aware of the importance of bringing mindfulness to situations, especially upsetting ones, he wished he could have responded to his son in a different way. "Son, I went to a lot of trouble to get you some coaching lessons but now hear you no longer want to invest your time in basketball. I feel playing a sport is good for you; however, if your heart is not in it, I will cancel the coaching sessions, and because you haven't started them, I should get the advance payment back.

I have written of a Zen student named Bizah and his Master who would go to the village once a week to have a special kind of tea at a small restaurant. On one occasion, Bizah said, "Look over there, Master. That man is so very selfish and uncaring. He has eaten all the food and left his wife with none."

"Bizah, remember you should not judge others," said his Master.

The next week when they went to the village for their teatime, the same man and his wife were there. The Master said, "Look at that man, Bizah. That man has eaten all the food. His wife has eaten nothing.

"Master, Bizah responded, "Last week you told me not to judge others and now you do so yourself. I am confused."

The Master responded, "A week ago, what you said was a judgment, Bizah. What I said today is not a judgment: it is a fact."

PRACTICE

Think of a time when you just "lost it". Play that time in your memory or write it down. What were the outcomes of that incident? How did you feel after?

Now, replay it in your mind or rewrite the scene coming from mindfulness. How did you change it? How would you have felt after?

8

INNER BODY MEDITATION

"Awareness of the inner body is consciousness remembering its origin and returning to Source."

Eckhart Tolle, author of *The Power of Now* and *A New Earth*

As you enter this chapter, be aware it will likely contain new information for most and is highly experiential. This chapter contains the important practice of Innerbody Meditation, so please take your time as you go through it.

LOST IN THE WORLD

We were born into this existence as pure souls, our souls being all the love and wisdom of our spiritual nature. In time, though, we needed to leave this pure innocence and awareness and enter "the outer world". As we did, we started to lose the memory of our true nature until, in time, we couldn't consciously remember it at all. The doors of the outside world started to close in on us. We began to experience this illusory world. Why illusory? Because it is based on the illusion of separation from our Source.

Day by day we became more consumed by the world of human experience: of felt separation, of egoic-driven need, of the compulsive draw of our sense perceptions, of limited and conditioned thinking, of emotional and physical pain. We became lost. We felt disillusioned and just wanted to find our way back home to our true Self.

The good news is that we can never lose who we truly are. Nor can we lose our home within our Source. This knowing still resides in our individual subconscious and universal consciousness, just waiting to surface again into our awareness. We get evidence of this when, at times, we feel the rapture of seeing the beauty of nature, are surprised by intense joy that has no apparent cause, experience unconditional love for and from another, feel deep gratitude for the many gifts we experience in our life, and a peace that surpasses understanding, meaning when we ask ourselves, "How can I be experiencing such deep peace in this troubling time?"

Depending upon how we travel through and learn from our human experiences, we will likely remain challenged in the current human condition until the body dies. To minimize and hopefully eliminate these challenges, we will try to find the way back to living from our true Self.

THE WAY BACK IS THROUGH THE BODY

How ironic that the way back to our original innocence requires us to return by re-entering the body in an attempt to reverse the process of just being "human".

When we enter the body through meditation that leads to stillness, we can hear in wordless silence our Source always guiding us back to It.

Just as our soul entered this world in a body, we need to use the body to exit it back to the realization of who we truly are. And the beautiful thing is that all of us carry this body around with us throughout our human life, so we always have immediate access to the awareness we hold within it.

It is through feeling the consciousness within our inner body that we then are able to feel the consciousness within all Life.

But HOW can we enter the body to reawaken the awareness of our true Self that has been there all along, just awaiting our recognition and appreciation of it?

WHAT IS INNER BODY MEDITATION?

The body is *in* the field of universal consciousness, yet at the same time paradoxically holds *within it* this consciousness. Mystics knew this for centuries – that the microcosm can contain the macrocosm or put more in this context, that the consciousness within the individual physical body, once awakened, brings us to a higher consciousness, which resides in the universal field of consciousness.

Within the individual physical body is a vibrant, alive energy body of consciousness. It is through inner body meditation that we can ignite the consciousness within it. When we come to experience the consciousness within us, we come to realize we are not just our physical body but inestimably more. Then the ego, which lives on a belief in smallness, fear, and separation begins to naturally diminish.

Inner body meditation involves entering the inner energy body, feeling it, and becoming one with the feeling so as to go *beyond* it in order to experience our formless true nature: joy, peace, love.

When learning the practice of inner body meditation, the steps are sequenced in a specific way so as to bring the meditator to full inner body awareness and through that to a higher level of consciousness. With ongoing practice, the meditator comes to a point when the felt awareness of consciousness within the inner body is a permanent state. They then live a life of Presence where their inner consciousness connects with the external world of mind formations and sense experiences. This will become clearer after you have experienced inner body meditation.

Inner body meditation takes us into a state of stillness. Stillness, as stated earlier, is no thought. By putting attention on the breath, igniting the inner energy body of consciousness through our intention and attention and holding our attention on the sensations of it, focus is taken away from the compulsive chatter of the mind.

Alfred Lord Tennyson in his poem "The Higher Pantheism", referring to God, said, "Closer is He than breathing, and nearer than hands and feet." What is closer to you than your breath? Your awareness of it. And what is closer to you than hands and feet? The animating life force of consciousness within them that Eckhart Tolle, world renowned author and spiritual teacher, calls "the inner body" that you can activate by giving your inner body your attention. Full attention is focused consciousness that ignites increased consciousness. This focused attention, when applied to parts or all of your inner body, ignites the consciousness that is already in the body but lays dormant until recognized by giving it our attention. What we have been searching for is already here – inside us!

THE BREATH WILL TAKE YOU INWARD

THE IMPORTANCE OF NATURAL BREATHING

Please put one of your hands on your upper chest and one on your belly. Notice from where you are breathing – the upper chest or belly? When you breathe only from your upper chest, you cannot take in as much oxygen as when you breathe from the belly to the upper chest. The upper chest can only expand to a small degree to take in oxygen, while the belly pushes out then down when breathing, allowing you to take in and exhale considerably more air. We often breathe only from the upper chest when we are in a state of stress or anxiety. Because of this, some refer to this kind of breathing as egoic breathing. Often when we see pictures or statues of the Buddha, he is depicted with a full round belly. Perhaps we are being told something from such images. Breathe from your belly. It is called natural breathing since it is how we should breathe. But we can also call it Buddha breathing.

PRACTICE

Put one hand on your belly, and for five minutes breathe naturally from there. Let the breath start from the belly and once it is full, let it rise up to the upper chest. If you are not used to breathing from your belly, you may want to start every sitting meditation by giving attention to this. Also, if you are not used to breathing naturally, when you start this, you may take in too much oxygen and feel dizzy. If this happens, decrease the amount of oxygen you take into the belly. Natural breathing is just that, natural and rhythmic, not exaggerated breathing.

SETTING UP FOR INNERBODY MEDITATION

When I refer to inner body meditation, I am referring to this meditation practice in general. When I join the words to form Innerbody Meditation, I am referring to the name of the course I teach.

Of course, it is hard to meditate on the inner body after just reading about the HOW to do this. For this reason, I suggest you read the following guided Innerbody Mediation a few times before practicing it yourself. Then visit my website, www.constancekellough.com and download for free an audio of this meditation with my leading you through it.

As a teacher of Innerbody Meditation, I know the importance of setting up to do this.

Sit upright in a chair with your spine erect. Make sure the body is comfortable, because if it is not, it will be distracting. Still the body.

In a sitting meditation, it is very difficult to enter a state of inner stillness if the body is not still.

Both feet should be planted firmly on the floor. Your legs should be hip width apart and slightly splayed. Put both of your hands on the middle of your thighs, palms facing downward – not too far forward, since you will then be stretching or not too close to your waist, since that will cause you to feel tight and your shoulders to rise. Keep your fingers slightly splayed as well.

Relax. Take a full natural breath in through the nose. Hold it to the count of four; then, exhale fully through the mouth, as if pushing the air out. If done correctly, you should hear your breath as you exhale. When you exhale, let your shoulders drop down, thereby relaxing the body. Do this twice more, each time letting your shoulders drop down further. Now continue to breathe naturally.

GUIDED INNERBODY MEDITATION, AS I TEACH IT

Set up for meditation as explained above.

With your hands palms down and eyes closed, how do you know that your right hand is there? Because you can feel the energy within it. It is often felt like a tingling sensation or vibration. This is the consciousness within your right hand. Keep feeling the sensation in your right hand.

Keeping your eyes closed, now take your focused attention to your left hand. Feel it come alive with energy because you have given it your attention. Keep feeling that sensation of your left hand.

Now put attention on both hands at the same time. Enjoy the sensation within your hands.

Now put your attention on your right foot. Ignite the energy in it by giving it your attention.

Now put your attention on the big toe of your right foot.

Experience that just because you singled out and gave attention to your big right toe, that it too began to feel more alive with energy. Feel the big toe and the rest of your right foot at the same time. Repeat this sequence with your left foot.

Check to see that you are continuing to breathe from the belly in a natural way.

Now feel both feet at the same time. Feel them heavy on the floor and grounded deep into Mother Earth.

Now focus your attention on your right lower leg, then left lower leg. Feel the inner energy of consciousness within them come alive. Then move your attention to your upper right leg, then to your upper left leg.

Take your time to awaken the areas you have given your attention to. Enjoy this felt experience of your Self.

While holding to feeling the energy in your hands, now feel at the same time the energy in your feet, your lower and upper legs.

Be gentle. Be easy. No efforting. Let everything go. Sense every part of the external body fall down, as if melting. Feel how wonderful it is to inhabit the body and feel your own sensation – the animating life force within you.

Now, ignite the energy of consciousness in your lower right arm. Then your lower left arm. Take whatever time you need to feel them come alive with the energy of consciousness.

Now, move your full attention to your right upper arm, then left upper arm.

Be easy. Be gentle. No efforting – just delight in the awakening of and the feeling of the consciousness within your upper arms.

Now awaken the whole of your lower back from the right side to the left. Check to make sure you are not holding yourself up from your lower back and buttock. Relax. Feel your sit bones sink into your chair.

Now to your shoulders. Check to make sure you are not holding them up. Let them stay relaxed and feeling they have fallen downward. We hold a lot of tension in our shoulders. Let that all go. Let your shoulders go unsupported and fall. Then feel the animating life force within them.

Move your attention to the middle of the back of the neck. This is where the spinal cord meets the brain stem. Ignite the energy of consciousness in this area.

Now, take in the whole neck. Give it your loving attention. Thank it for supporting your spine and holding your head up.

We now will move up to the face where all 5 of our outer senses reside. The face has many nerves in it and is very sensitive, making it easier for you to feel the energy in it.

Put your attention on your nose. It may help to first feel the energy of the tip of your nose then to the nostrils before you move to the complete nose.

It is difficult to feel your individual eyes and to try to do so causes you to strain. Therefore, think you are wearing an eye mask and feel the energy in that whole area – from ear to ear.

Now, move to the mouth. We use the mouth so often and the lips are highly sensitive. You should be able to feel your lips come alive with the energy of consciousness very quickly.

Now, ignite the energy in your right outer ear. Then move to ignite it in the inner ear canal as well. Do the same with the left ear.

Now, focusing more on the interior of your ears, adopt a listening attitude. This is important because, as previously mentioned, this can create and feel like a vacuum, so to speak, which invites higher universal consciousness to be received.

Now ignite the energy in your forehead. When you do this, consciousness may direct your attention to the third eye area between the eye brows and about an inch above them. If so, you may feel the area of the third eye becoming very active, even intense as it starts to awaken or open further. If this is the case and becomes uncomfortable, move on to the next step in this practice.

Now take your attention to your scalp. We also hold a lot of tension in our scalp, which is one of the reasons we experience headaches. Let all that tension in the scalp dissolve as ice in warm water.

Now feel the whole head: chin, lips, nose, ears, eye area, forehead and scalp as one energy field.

You are now ready to feel the whole of your body as one unified field of energy. Take your time to do this. Enjoy the sensation of your Self. Now, figuratively speaking, turn up the intensity dial to increase the vibrational frequency of consciousness in your whole body. You can do this simply by your intention to do so.

Abide in the sensation of the inner body as long as you want.

Then give thanks for coming to know through this experience the consciousness you hold within you.

DEBRIEFING YOUR INNERBODY MEDITATION EXPERIENCE

Being able to share one's experience in a group and ask questions with a live teacher is best. However, given the limitations of writing about Innerbody Meditation, I will share with you some of the most common Innerbody meditators' experiences with explanations.

Student: I felt certain parts of my body get very warm.
Teacher: That means an awakening and or expansion of consciousness within these parts of your body. Enjoy the warmth and give thanks for it.

S: I felt my body become cold. I needed to go put on my jacket. I never get cold.

T: You can feel cold when you are integrating the awakened part of consciousness within the body that has always been there but not known or felt until you gave it your attention. Appreciate and give thanks for this.

S: I feel more comfortable when I cross my legs.

T: Then cross your legs. Being physically comfortable is important. Some say they feel more relaxed when they just rest their open palms on their thighs. Then they should do just that.

S: I felt pain in my arm.

S: I felt pain in my neck.

T: Whenever you awaken consciousness within the body, there is some kind of reaction. On the physical level this is often felt as a pain. As you keep your conscious attention on that area - without going into thought - it will soften and go away. Did that happen for you?

S: Yes.

S: Yes.

S: I felt nauseous in my stomach and solar plexus areas.

T: That is likely because you have held some emotional pain in those areas that you weren't aware of until you put your attention into the body. Just hold your conscious attention there, while also being an observer. The nausea will get weaker or dissipate.

S: I felt an uncomfortable restriction in my chest.

T: The chest is where we hold strong attachments. These attachments are always related to me and mine. They could be attachments to your parents, a lost lover, your money, your reputation, and so forth. This is an indication to look at what you are attached to that may be holding you back from feeling freer.

S: Some strong emotion came up from my past which made me feel very uncomfortable.

T: Give the emotion your conscious attention. Feel it and witness it at the same time; then, drop it into your stomach. Barry Long, now deceased but one of the few masters of inner body meditation, said that the stomach plays two roles. It digests food and turns it into vital energy to run the physical body, but its second function is to burn up, to digest any unhealthy or unwelcomed emotion in you. When you feel an unwanted emotion or even an unwelcomed thought, drop it into the stomach area where it will be "burned up" in your "inner oven", meaning it will be neutralized, rendered benign, or transmuted into consciousness. [1]

S: My back pain, which I have had for years, is gone.
T: That is because by igniting the consciousness within your back, the consciousness held within that area brought about a healing or temporary relief. Don't enter Innerbody Meditation with an expectation to experience some kind of physical healing, although that may occur. There is so much more going on when you awaken the consciousness within – at all levels: physical, mental, emotional, and spiritual. Enter and practice Innerbody Meditation with the intention of experiencing your true Self.

S: I felt my hands get very heavy.
T: That's because when you awakened the consciousness within them, you also became aware of your physical hands resting on your knees and felt the weight of them. Getting in touch with your inner

body assists you to become more sensitive to and get in touch with your physical body as well. In addition, because you have relaxed your shoulders, upper, and lower arms and let everything just "fall down", so to speak, this could have contributed to your hands feeling heavy.

S: I felt the energy in my throat area get stronger and stronger, even though I didn't put my attention there.

T: This is because the awakened consciousness wanted to ignite the consciousness in your throat chakra. It is amazing how the intelligence of consciousness, once activated, keeps the awakening and healing process going without our even intending it. Does this make sense to you? Have you had challenges speaking to others, speaking your truth?

S: Yes.

S: I saw blue cloud-like formations come and go.

S: I saw bright lights flashing.

S: I saw a huge flame emerge then pass away.

T: This kind of phenomenon is quite common. Just observe such visuals. Don't try to create them, interpret them, nor avoid them. These are just indicators of the expression of consciousness at play within your Being.

S: It takes quite a long time to do a full Innerbody Meditation. I don't know if I can find enough time every day to do this.

T: Yes, at first this form of meditation takes time as you learn how to and practice animating your inner body. However, once you have continued in this for some time, you will be able to enter your inner energy body at will. You will sit and with your intention to do so be immediately in the body. And if you continue in this meditative practice, there will come a time when you don't even have to will feeling the sensation of your inner body. You will have "embodied" it, so to speak. As such, you will be able to carry this gift with you wherever you go for the rest of your life, so giving extra time when you start practicing Innerbody Meditation is well worth it. Also see Appendix A.

S: I felt the energy within my inner body and was able to observe it as well as it moved from place to place. Then when I went back to just focusing on the sensation within my body, I felt I became one with the sensation. There was no separation.
T: Wonderful.

Innerbody Meditation is the portal to opening and experiencing the fullness of consciousness within the body, the consciousness that you are.

As we put attention on our breath, we take it away from the thinking mind. This happens too when we put our attention on the tingling, electrifying sensation of the inner body once we have ignited the consciousness within it.

When entering a state of both stillness and sensation through Innerbody Meditation, we can also become aware of the spaciousness within us. As with external space that is not empty, the space within the inner body is filled with energy. When our eyes are closed, we see a kind of grainy background that holds both light and the dark. Look into this inner space that has no boundaries. Your true Self as well has no boundaries. When you go deep into Innerbody Meditation, you may come to a time when you will have gone beyond sensation: you won't feel your external body nor your inner body – just the fullness of your Being that is non-physical and beyond space and time. This state feels both empty and full at the same time. Enjoy resting in your true Being.

Through Innerbody Meditation we also open ourselves to experiencing the states of our Being. Instead of only rarely, we will then experience them more often and in greater intensity in our lives. Put Innerbody Meditation to the test and see how your life and your approach to life improves.

It's through Innerbody Meditation, we come to know the power of consciousness we hold within. After such an experience, it is more difficult to go back to seeing ourselves as vulnerable beings having to fear so many things. And without being fearful, the ego cannot hold us hostage.

So now we can update 17th Century philosopher Renee Descartes. How do I know I exist? Not because "I think therefore I am" but because "I *sense* my Self therefore I am."

9

PRESENCE

"It is only by grounding our awareness in the living sensation of our bodies that the 'I Am', our real presence, can be awakened."

G. I. Gurdjieff

WHAT IS PRESENCE?

Now that you know about and have practiced Innerbody Meditation, you are prepared to understand what Presence is. It is when you hold to the felt inner body of consciousness and at the same time are present with your outer senses in the world. When you do this, you bring consciousness into whatever you are currently experiencing. In an uncomfortable or conflict situation, immediately go into your inner body. Stay present inside and out. Hold to Presence. Then let the situation unfold. When coming from Presence, we can be assured that by bringing our attention to the outside situation we will influence it for the better: it will be healing, improve a situation, and will dissolve conflict, at least to some degree. What a powerful treasure we hold within us. It can be likened somewhat to having a spiritual inner wand to draw upon and use.

But don't wait for an uncomfortable, intense experience to trigger you to go into the inner energy body. Do it as often as you can in ordinary situations such as checking out in the grocery line, greeting the bus driver, speaking with your server at a restaurant. If you do it regularly in such ordinary times, it will build up your "Presence musculature", so to speak. It will become your way of being in the world. No intention will be needed, you will just be the consciousness of love.

PRACTICE

When you next meet a problematic or uncomfortable situation or person, go immediately into Presence and communicate from this energy field. Turn up the intensity dial of the vibration of energy through your intention to do so. There is no judgment, no reactivity – just extended Presence. Note what happens.

PRACTICE

The next time you sit with someone in private conversation, hold to the inner energy body. Speak and listen from full inner body awareness, from Presence. Did you notice a difference in how the conversation went? Did it feel "deeper"? Did you notice a stronger connection with the person you were talking to? Did you get any indication the other person felt there was something different in your conversing with them this time?

It has been said that one morning in what was then called Calcutta, India, Mother Teresa and her Sisters of Charity were running late for their visit to the first clinic on their daily rounds. As the cadre of nuns hurried along the streets of Calcutta that morning, Mother suddenly stopped in her tracks. Turning to her right, she looked down at a curb piled with street-side garbage. Walking over to the curb, she bent down. Out of the trash, she picked up a discarded premature infant, so small she could cradle it in the palm of one of her hands. The infant was in the crunched-up fetal position. As Mother Theresa gazed with love at this wee and weak creature, the infant moved one arm then the other, one foot then the other, gradually opening fully like a flower to the warmth of Mother's love.

This story is sometimes recounted to show the power of the inclusive, unconditional love Mother Teresa extended wherever she went. I suggest that there is another important lesson to be gleaned from this incident.

The practice of the Sisters of Charity was to spend two hours at the beginning of each day in prayer and stillness. On this particular morning, they had spent more than the allotted time, which is why they were running late. Had Mother Teresa not spent so much time in stillness, would she have had the inner Presence to be alerted to the tiny manifestation of Presence by the side of the road?

And again, because our Source extends equally to all, we know this same Presence is within everyone, even though they may not yet be in touch with it, aware of it. When we live from Presence, we live from a higher state of awareness. Because of this, we are connected to and can feel the Presence in everyone and everything. We come to see the other as *our Self*.

When people join in a state of Presence, there is Oneness. This is what the word "Namaste" in one of its extended definitions means: "I honor the place in you in which the entire universe dwells. I honor the place in you which is of love, of truth, of light, and of peace. When you are in that place in you, and I am in that place in me, *we are one*."

If you have only one or two people in a group who hold to Presence, it will affect the whole group. This is the power of an authentic spiritual teacher. Coming from a deep well of Presence, they invite others to join them there.

When you meet a true spiritual teacher, you can *feel* their energy, their powerful essence. To be in their presence is not only welcomed but transformative because your essence is further awakened by being drawn into theirs. It's not only the words an authentic spiritual teacher speaks that carry power, but more importantly their very Presence that flows energetically through their words. That is why many can teach using words, but there are few who teach using words that ignite the truth within you.

This is likely why, on the collective level, when those we have deemed "great in Spirit" pass on and their form is no longer with us, their essence is freed to be fully expressed and picked up by as many who energetically resonate with it, whether alive at the time of their passing or those born in subsequent generations – and perhaps for thousands of years thereafter.

It is curious that often who a person truly is becomes best known, becomes more impactful to others once their form has died. It is as if the vehicle of the body restricted who they were in their most authentically powerful Self.

The power of Presence in just one individual can be seen in Herman Hess' *Journey to the East*. It is the story of various individuals who join together in a temporary community to go on a pilgrimage.

Their destination is purposely not mentioned by Hess, as he does not see that as important in terms of a focus in the story. Initially everything goes smoothly. The pilgrims get along together and cover a good distance every day.

The reader is soon introduced to a simple, quiet, happy, and unaffected fellow named Leo who always seems to be around at the right time, cheerfully helping out in whatever manner he can. There is something so pleasing and welcoming about Leo that everyone loves his presence.

Then one day Leo suddenly disappears without explanation. "Where did Leo go?" is the burning question. "And how could he leave without telling us?" A search party is formed to try to find him, but to no avail.

With Leo gone, relationships between the pilgrims become strained. Bickering and arguing break out, then accelerate.

The narrator, who the reader assumes is Hess himself, soon loses interest in the pilgrimage and his quest. He abandons the group but carries with him an obsession to know more about Leo and the reason for his sudden departure.

This takes him on his own journey, a solo pilgrimage during which, no matter where he visits, he is always on the lookout for Leo and never abandons the hope that they will someday meet again.

A number of years pass before he stumbles across a lead: the name Andreas Leo, given to him by a person who is helping him with research on a project. The narrator sets out to discover whether this indeed could be the Leo he has been searching for all along. When he locates Andreas Leo, he stops him on the street, and they engage in conversation. Yes, this is the Leo who left the pilgrimage group so many years earlier, but he does not recognize the narrator. Leo has to get back to his work, and the two part company. Only later does the narrator find out that the unassuming Leo is actually President of the League that sponsored the pilgrimage in the first place.

The reader, like the actual pilgrims, becomes aware that Leo has something special within him that has such a positive influence on others—an ability to bring very different people together for a common purpose. Robert Greenleaf, in *Servant Leadership*, attributes Leo's positive influence on others to the fact that he played a servant role within the group. The evolution of our consciousness now tells us that additionally the "something very special" in Leo was his Presence. Exuding a strong field of Presence, he drew this same Presence out in the other pilgrims.

On several occasions, I have shared this story when giving talks, encouraging participants to leave the workshop as Leos, bringing their healing Presence into our world.

This powerful aura of Presence has been referred to in the East as the "Buddha field". But we don't need to wait to sit with a teacher in order to benefit from this field. We need only recognize and cultivate our own inner Presence and *be* this Presence in the world.

Bring Presence into your everyday life. An important meeting is before you; a key decision needs to be made soon; you feel wobbly after a crisis hits; a situation has arisen unexpectedly and you don't know how to respond. Go into your body and ignite the energy of consciousness within it so as to come from a state of Presence.

10

THE TREASURES WITHIN OUR BODY

"Inside your body is a shrine.
Inside the shrine is the lotus flower.
Inside the lotus flower is a tiny space.
Inside that tiny space lives the Creator.
Inside the Creator is the Universe.
Find it, and you will be one with the Creator and all things.
Be there, and all things and the Creator will be one with you."

A passage from the UPANISHADS, the Sacred scriptures of India.

We have been told that our real treasures lie within us. Many of us keep seeking but not finding them. Is it because we have never been shown HOW to do this?

Let's explore this body of ours.

As previously stated, it will likely seem contradictory at first to hear that we are not our body, then to say that it is the consciousness found within the body that is the avenue to finding out who we truly are. Imagine: we have been living in this physical form since birth but for the most part have not explored the treasures within it.

Our 5 physical senses serve as tools for our experiences by bringing us information from our environment. Precious and needed they are, but like magnets also pull us into the external world. As mentioned, it is our sense of sight that has the greatest capacity to do this. That is why when we go inward to meditate or pray, we usually close our eyes. It is also the reason why we do the same when listening attentively to beautiful music. In addition, we often cover our eyes when something on TV, in the movies or real life are things we don't want to take in.

Our outer senses can mislead us if through them we come to believe the exterior world is the only important or most important thing, not realizing that the external is a creation of our state of consciousness. If we want to change some of our life experiences, we must go within, which is where we find the cause of them. Our experiences are always created from the inside out. Even what we take in with our outer senses, comes from our inner awareness we have at a particular time.

OUR NON-PHYSICAL SENSES

In addition to our physical senses, we have non-physical, inner senses that are of a higher order of consciousness, of knowing. Emanuel Swedenborg referred to these as our spiritual senses.[1]

- Hearing – to become aware of higher truth or heart-felt sincerity. "I hear you."
- Sight – understanding something you haven't before. Spiritual insight. That "Aha" experience. "I see."
- Touch – to have a heart-felt experience, to be deeply moved or

appreciative. "I am touched."

· Smell – when you are questioning if the milk in the fridge is still fresh enough to be safe to drink, you take it out and smell it. Before you taste it, you usually smell it. Has it gone bad or not? Similarly, through your inner sense of smell, you can tell if a certain person is someone to spend time with or move away from or if a situation tells you to embrace it or find the exit door – and quickly. For example, when you are around a genuinely loving person, they "smell" good.

· Taste – lets us know if something is good, if it feels right or true. When you enjoy learning something, it tastes good. Spiritual truth tastes good.

You may have often asked someone, especially children, how they knew a certain thing. "How do you know that?" They often answer, "I don't know. I just know." When we experience something through our non-physical senses, it comes with a sense of certainty.

Our consciousness at any one time affects what we see and understand. Most of us have had the experience of reading a book, especially a spiritual book, then going back and reading it again after a year or so. When reading it for the second time, we see and understand so many more things. The book has a greater depth to it for us now. The words in the book have not changed, but our level of consciousness has changed between the first and second reading.

When we steer through life only using our outer senses, logic, and worldly experiences, we do not experience on an internal basis – things as they really are on a more subtle consciousness level. In ignoring the spiritual, non-tangible inner life, we are missing out on experiencing the guiding force of the intelligence within us that brings immense security and meaning to our lives.

If we want to grow spiritually, we will benefit by being attentive to what our non-physical senses are communicating to us. It is partly through them that we develop intuition, precognition, insights and creative ideas.

THE WAND OF CONSCIOUSNESS

In Joseph McMoneagle's autobiographical account, *Memoirs of a Psychic Spy*, he relates how his inner knowing from "his gut", as he puts it, kept him from death during his stint in the Vietnam War.

In this time of great danger, when every cell in his body had to be on full alert, he was forced into present moment awareness. Here he heard the unquestionable guidance from his non-physical senses. He writes:

> What is material about my time in Vietnam is how much I came to rely on my gut or intuitive nature. Many times I instinctively knew I wasn't safe, or that I was somehow exposed to danger. The small voice inside my gut became a lot louder and I listened. Inside and outside the base camp, I always listened to my inner voice, did whatever it suggested, and did it without question. If I felt an urge to get into a bunker, I did so immediately. If it was a gut feeling to zig rather than zag, then that's what I did. I once abandoned a Jeep and walked back to the base camp on advice of my internal voices. To the consternation of my first sergeant, the Jeep was never seen again.

While sitting in a listening post one night near a small unit outside of Tay Ninh, I had a terrible urge to move. The small voice in my gut was telling me to be anywhere but there. Movement was difficult because it was pitch black—the kind of dark where you can't see your hand right up in front of your face. I had to convince the two others who were there it was the right thing to do. It took almost an hour, but we shifted west of our original position by about sixty yards. Around 4:00 a.m. we heard a series of grenades going off in the area we had previously occupied. [2]

What is evident about this account is that McMoneagle did not doubt, question, or second guess his inner senses—an indication that he had already built a trusting relationship with them. His experiences of the saving power of his inner knowing encourage us not to wait until a time of extreme personal danger to start developing these inner senses, which until now for many of us have either remained latent or only communicating with us at partial capacity. Once we have shed the self-imposed limitation of only thinking, we are able to access these higher levels of knowing.

THE INTELLIGENCE OF THE HUMAN HEART

The heart is the first organ to form in the body. Although it pumps approximately 1,900 gallons of blood a day, it is not simply a pump. It is vastly more.

Normally when we speak of someone being intelligent, we are referring to their level of knowledge they can express from their rational thinking mind. But what about the wisdom of the heart? The body is electromagnetic. That's why it cannot live long without water as a conductor. The heart is the strongest electromagnetic force in the body. It is 70-100 times electrically stronger and up to 5,000 times magnetically stronger than the brain. [3] The heart, with its approximately 40,000 neurons, has its own "brain system", so to speak, although it doesn't contain any brain cells. You can *know* with your heart.

The heart has memory. Long after we may have forgotten something, the heart maintains the feeling around that person or incident. In some heart transplants, recipients took on some of the temperament characteristics, habits and even food preferences and cravings of their donors.

The heart sends signals to the brain and the brain to the heart, but the brain receives fewer signals than the heart. The heart signals to the brain what kind of hormones and chemicals should be released in the body. When we access intelligence or non-thinking awareness through the heart, it then sends a signal to the brain to interpret it. Our mind may wander often, but a healthy heart is always alert.

Our emotions and feelings affect the electromagnetic field around the heart and this field affects what is around us – individuals, plants, animals, and even machinery. When we come from our heart, when we come from love, we join with another or others and if we are physically close to them, meaning within 5-8 feet in all directions, we even have a positive influence on *their* electromagnetic field. [4]

The heart even acts as a hormone gland giving off oxytocin, the hormone of love. This gland is especially active when a mother gives birth to a child.

The Institute of Heart Math is continuing its pioneering research into the role, intelligence, and power of the heart. When our mind and heart are unified, they function together optimally. They are then said to be in coherence. This coherence means there is an extended neuro network at work. When we harmonize the signals the heart gives off with our brain waves, we create positive and healing emotions such as appreciation and compassion. There is a feeling of calm and safety evoked, dissipating the fight or flight reaction when we are under stress.

We can create heart-brain coherence very quickly. [5]

PRACTICE
Create heart-brain coherence by putting your right hand on your heart area, thereby bringing your immediate attention to this area. Slow your breathing. When you breathe slowly, you send a signal to your entire body that you are safe. The body, in turn, invites you to turn inward. Breathe as if your breath is coming into and out from your heart.

Fill your heart with a positive emotion for yourself or someone else such as love, gratitude, compassion. Activate the full energy of this feeling. Embrace and intensify this feeling. Hold to this feeling. The longer you can hold to this feeling, the stronger the communication and coherence is between your heart and your brain.

People are more aware today of the role the heart plays in fostering unity consciousness because it resonates love that joins with other people and all living things. The thinking mind, bound tightly with the ego, sees only separation. Is that why many are now being drawn to find out the power and wisdom of the heart – because the heart leads to evolution through realized Oneness, yet the limited thinking mind and its strong companion the ego lead to separation thinking and therefore threaten devolution?

THE INTELLIGENCE OF CONSCIOUSNESS
THROUGHOUT THE ENTIRE BODY

There is now evidence that the solar plexus is an essential part of our nervous system. Indeed, it acts as another brain in the body. [6]

The solar plexus contains a complex network of nerves. Like the heart, it receives and transmits nerve impulses to the brain – and perhaps to the heart as well. The latter has yet to be confirmed. Some have called it our "feeling brain". We all have had those strong feelings in our gut that guide us or inform us in some way. Whether we follow its promptings, its wisdom is up to us.

It is interesting that the heart and the solar plexus are also 2 of the centers of the body's 7 major chakras. One day we may find that all the 7 major chakra areas have their own purposeful knowing, intelligence. If so, what about the other 20 less dominant chakras in the body?

Of the approximately 70-100 trillion cells in the body, each emits a bio-photonic light that is so rarefied that it cannot be seen by the human eye. Yet it is there, emanating the light from the life of each cell. As mentioned earlier, each of the cells in our body has a specific function to serve other cells and be served by them. There must be significant intelligence in each of them to guide and assure such a process.

Going back to Sri Aurobindo, Teilhard de Chardin, and Apostle St. Paul referred to earlier, each one saw the body as being the bridge to higher consciousness. Sri Aurobindo saw humanity in a transitional state, a temporary state that would be supplanted because the body would finally be rescued from the illusions and oppression of the egoic-driven mind. He envisioned spiritual light and realization filling the cells of the body. Sri Aurobindo felt a heightened form of consciousness, when embodied by a sufficient number of people, would start a contagion of consciousness that would spread throughout humanity. St Paul called this evolutionary leap the "Resurrection". As individuals begin to look within the body and ignite the consciousness within it, which previously had mainly remained dormant, St. Paul thought we will witness an awakening and progressive resurrection of the body into light.

11

FURTHER EXPLORATION INTO THE INTELLIGENCE WITHIN THE BODY

In the guided meditation practice presented in Chapter 8, we were working with the consciousness held in the inner energy body. Let's turn our attention now to awakening and balancing the energy within the subtle or the non-physical body where we experience different aspects of higher consciousness.

THE CHAKRAS

Chakras are concentrated energy centers of the subtle, non-physical body. The subtle body is connected intimately with the physical body and vice-versa.

In summary, there are 7 major chakras within the subtle body but also 20 other sub-major chakras that regulate the life energy flow within the body. These are within the body but not physical; they are energy centers. When the chakras spin, they draw in energy from the universal life force. They are receivers and transmitters of the subtle, more refined energy of consciousness, the universal life force.

Because most of you reading this book are already familiar with the 7 major chakras, I will not go into detail here. For those who aren't, you can get immediate and lengthy information on them in other books and from an internet search.

The 7 major chakras are each associated with one or more of the endocrine glands that secrete hormones directly into the blood. In ancient India they did not know this. Now modern India and the metaphysical, medical, and scientific fields have found this out. The chakras process the subtle energy of consciousness then bring this to the physical endocrine glands and nervous system and from them to specific areas of our physical body. There is a back and forth communication between the chakras and the endocrine glands and nervous system. All the chakras and endocrine glands are important for overall health, wellbeing, and the development of human consciousness.

"Chakra" means wheel. Each of the 7 major chakras is cone-shaped and spins clockwise, with the wide opening at the front of the body and the smaller opening at the back of the body. When a chakra is healthy, it is not blocked, spins harmoniously and aids in keeping us healthy spiritually, emotionally, physically, and mentally. Because the chakras work together as a harmonious system, a block in one can put the others out of balance. When a chakra is out of balance, it is slow in turning and the energy it gives off to serve the body is weakened.   When one or more of the chakras are slowed, usually because of constant daily stress on the physical, mental, and emotional bodies, this indicates an obstruction of energy flow, that can lead to an imbalance or illness of some sort. The last line of defense is the physical body, so we want to correct any imbalance before it turns into a physical ailment.

PRACTICE

The following is a way to balance your 7 major chakras. You can utter these "seed" sounds to yourself in silence or out loud. If you are in a situation where you can tone them out loud, this is preferable, since the energy from verbally toning is stronger. If you go to my website, www.constancekellough.com, you can join me in toning these "seed" sounds out loud. The best approach is to balance all the chakras, since we don't know which, if any, is out of balance and affecting a weakening in the others.

CHAKRA PURIFICATION PROCESS

This Process has been taken from *Health – It's All About Consciousness* by Ivan Rados.

For this Process, our breathing will be deep and full, breathing from the belly to the top of the rib cage. As we chant the sounds, we should open up to both the resonance of the voice and the vibration in the body where the particular chakra spins. It is suggested that you remain in silence for a minute or two between the toning for each chakra.

Following is the list of "seed" sounds that access and ignite the elemental qualities of each chakra.

LAM FOR THE ROOT CHAKRA

Curve the tip of your tongue up and back, placing it on the rear section of the upper palate to pronounce a sound like the word "alum", without the initial "a".

VAM FOR THE NAVAL CHAKRA

Place your upper teeth on the inner section of your lower lip and begin with a breathy consonant to imitate the sound of a fast-moving car. Pronounce the mantra like "fvam".

RAM FOR THE SOLAR PLEXUS CHAKRA

Place the tip of your tongue on the roof of the front section of your upper palate; roll the "r" and pronounce the mantra like the first part of the world "rum-ble".

YAM FOR THE HEART CHAKRA

Pronounce the sound like the word "yum" (as in yummy).

HAM FOR THE THROAT CHAKRA

Pronounce the world "hum" (as in humming). Allow the breath to extend beyond the resolution of the consonant.

OM FOR THE THIRD EYE CHAKRA

Pronounce the sound as a barely audible whisper, allowing the sound and the breath to resonate in the cranial area.

AH FOR THE CROWN CHAKRA

Pronounce the AH by forming the sound near the rear of the palate.[1]

Everything is vibration, so the chakras which are forms of vibration, quickly respond to the vibration of our voice.

THE AURIC BODY

We have an auric or sometimes called our etheric body made up of 7 layers, one layer for each of the 7 major chakras. Each of the auric levels is governed by a specific chakra, but all chakras influence each layer. The chakras energize the auric body and regulate the flow of energy between its layers. Traditionally, we were told our aura surrounds our physical body and extends 2 inches to 3 feet from it. But now, based on the principles of physics, all energy fields are unbounded, meaning our aura, a bio-magnetic human energy field, can extend indefinitely.[2]

Whether consciously or unconsciously, we can feel someone's aura when we are near to them. Some individuals have the gift of seeing auras. Sometimes a person, when in tune with another, especially through love, can feel the other's aura even when separated by a great distance.

INTELLIGENCE AT THE CELLULAR LEVEL

We now know there are an estimated 70-100 trillion specialized cells within the body — each one cooperating with each other; each one serving and being served by each other. Our cells are on duty 24/7 and never rest. The cell, being a physical unit of communication, has been evolving for almost 4 billion years and is likely the beginning of natural intelligence.

The interconnected network of approximately 70 - 100 trillion cells within the body means each cell responds to change, has memory, can sense, and decide how it will function, and act — meaning it can problem-solve. They can recognize cells that are the same as them and those that are different. Each cell is surrounded by a membrane that enables it to see, hear, feel, and interpret messages that come in chemical form. [3] Cells communicate with other cells, so they have a language. They have an intelligence that enables them to collaborate with molecules and genes. They originate the communication from cells to molecules to genes. [4]

Although cells communicate with other cells, it is not yet known how they communicate within themselves. It has been argued that the intelligence within the cell goes beyond conventional modeling. It is an intelligence that is unrecognized to date by science and is not amenable to computer analysis. [5]

Even though we don't know how to communicate to cells via their own language, because cells are living, sensing bodies, we can communicate to them our love and appreciation which will be picked up by them at the vibrational level. All life forms respond to our loving attention, appreciation, and gratitude. Take, for examples, our plants, our pets, living trees, flowers, other humans.

PRACTICE
Go into the inner body. Activate it. Take some quiet time to sit and give appreciation and gratitude to your cells. Thank them for doing the amazing job of keeping you alive and working so hard for your well-being.

Quantum physics, which deals with things at the subatomic level, shows us a world in which nothing is solid. Everything is made up of an electromagnetic field of waves at different frequencies. Even though we cannot see the bio-photonic light made up of frequency waves, each cell gives off, it is there. Our bodies are filled with light or put another way, we are bodies of light! The light that Sri Arobindo, Saint Paul, and Teilhard de Chardin have referred to is real and already in us, and like the inner energy body, is it just awaiting our recognition of it?

12

EMBRACING OUR ONENESS

*"It really boils down to this: that all life is interrelated.
We are all caught within an interrelated network of mutuality, tied
into a single garment of destiny...We aren't going to have peace
on Earth until we recognize this basic fact of the interrelated
structure of all reality."*

Martin Luther King, Jr. – from "A Christmas Sermon on Peace", 1967

WE ARE SO MUCH ALIKE

Individual humans are truly so much alike, yet each a unique
expression of our Oneness. For most of us, before we can consider
being One, we first need to recognize our similarities. Dr. David
Berceli, one of the world's foremost field traumatologists, in his
book *The Revolutionary Trauma Release Process* recalls one of his
experiences of two realizing they are not that different at all.
As Berceli recounts:

> I was asked to go to Sudan to work with a Muslim and
> Christian population in the city of Khartoum. The
> invitation was from a nonprofit organization. I was

to work with two people who were co-leaders in the organization.

I began by hearing about the animosity between the two individuals, which was typically reflective of their culture.

"We are experiencing division that we believe is coming from our culture and not from us individually," said one of the participants. "Even though we want to move beyond these divisions, our animosity is so deeply entrenched that we don't seem to be able to pull ourselves out of it."

"If it's coming from the culture," I explained, "then you need to have a shared experience that restores your commonality as human beings."

I offered to lead them through such an experience, and they agreed to participate.

"How, in your bodies, do you know you are experiencing animosity?" I asked. "What exactly does it feel like?"

"I feel like my chest is tight, and I don't breathe deeply because I'm not relaxed," said one of the participants. "My shoulders are tight, my neck is tense, and I have a lot of anxiety in my body that I can't release."

The other was shocked to hear what his fellow worker

was experiencing. "That's exactly how I feel!" he exclaimed.

"You are having a common experience because all humans feel separation and division by means of an identical bodily process," I explained. "What you are both doing is separating yourselves from your bodies. The way to change this is for both of you to have an identical bodily experience that is positive."

At this point, I invited them to do the Trauma Release Process ™ I developed. I positioned them so they could both see each other doing the exercises. When they both began to tremor part way into the exercises, they realized that their bodies were responding in the same manner.

"What's going on in your body right now?" I asked.

The first man said, "I can feel my legs are tremoring from my feet up to my hips."

"Wow!" said the second man. "That's exactly what's happening to me."

This second man then described a different sensation. "I find myself tremoring in my stomach," he said. "At the same time, I am also beginning to feel my breath deepening."

"The identical sensation is happening in me," said the

second man.

"Yes, our bodies are responding in exactly the same way," agreed the other.

These two men were actually mirroring each other. I kept them tremoring against the wall for quite a while so they could experience how their bodies were acting in concert with each other.

"Your bodies are discharging the identical tension you were experiencing in your work together," I explained.

"My God," they both exclaimed, "we are so alike!"

Once I was able to get them to see that they were alike, it dismantled their conceptualization that they were so different. The animosity was now no longer there because they recognized they were essentially very similar to one another.

Once they restored a sense of their commonality, I had them lie on the floor for the final exercise. The tremors that arose from this exercise evoked laughter in both men to the point that they ended up with deep belly laughs. When they at last stood, they hugged each other, aware that they no longer had any sensation of animosity in their bodies.

There was nothing to work through, no deep analysis required. They simply needed to discharge what had been put onto them by their culture. [1]

CONNECTING THROUGH COMPASSION, NOT FEAR

Do you recall the sense of oneness that emerged all around the world on the day the Twin Towers in New York City collapsed? On every continent, millions came together in common grief, sensing that what was happening to the people of New York was in some way also happening to them. The 9/11 attacks spawned an ocean of compassion and goodwill toward the United States.

A few days after the 9/11 attacks on the World Trade Center, a colleague of mine was on his regular train commute home from New York City. The commuters were deep into their own worlds—reading newspapers, emailing from their then popular Blackberries, staring out of the windows, nodding off. As the sky turned an ominous dark gray, suddenly, there were loud bomb-like sounds. Coming on the heels of the attack on the Twin Towers, the explosive sounds startled everyone. The passengers, believing themselves to be targets of terrorists, were instantly abuzz with consternation. Complete strangers, shaken out of their isolation, were reaching out to whoever was nearby, questioning what was happening or reassuring each other. Just then the heavens opened up, signaling that the booms and darkening sky were caused by an imminent thunderstorm. As precipitously as the chatter had arisen, it ceased, and the commuters retreated once again into their isolated worlds.

My colleague commented how sad he felt that people, when frightened, spontaneously reached out to one another yet withdrew their presence just as quickly once they realized their fear was unfounded. He then started wondering what it would take for people to come together *without* the catalyst of fear.

Notice how we join with another with ease when we find something in common that we love, whether it be a love of a sport, children, country, golf, or gardening. This also suggests what we must do on the collective level if we are to go beyond our differences: identify what we value in common. It could be love of Mother Earth, support of the feminine principle, care for children in poverty and the oppressed, or a combination of such human values. Is this the answer my friend was seeking on his train commute home from New York City shortly after the attacks of 9/11? Was he not aware or did he forget many people *do* come together out of concern for their fellow humans, even though they may not know them personally?

EVIDENCE OF ONENESS

PERSONAL EXPERIENCES

The evidence of Oneness is strongly seen in our personal experiences. This can be confirmed by such things as when a mother intuitively knows her child is in danger and it proves to be so; the times you are about to say something to your partner, and your partner says the exact thing before you do; the time you had a novel idea or personal inspirational breakthrough only to have your close friend or a newspaper article echo this back to you the next day; the telephone rings and you know who it is before you pick it up; you travel to a faraway country and in a restaurant find your nearby neighbor having dinner at the table next to you. Indeed, many synchronous and seemingly improbable coincidences are evidence of our Oneness.

You may recall an afternoon you felt upset for no apparent reason, only to find out a day later that one of your dear friends was in a serious car accident. Once we make a connection, especially a deep connection with another or others, it is as if we are thereafter connected on "the circuit board" of life.

Compassion gives evidence of our Oneness. Notice how we can relate to and genuinely participate in the grief of another we have learned of from TV or the newspaper. Notice once we have experienced a particular health challenge, how closely we feel to those who have experienced the same.

Feel how another can affect our energy body, how they can replenish it, balance it, drain it, give it a negative or positive energy charge.

When we greet another from a state of Presence, if they are coming from Presence as well, we can quickly connect with the Presence within them. Also, this is why when two people on the same level of consciousness meet for the first time, it is as if they are meeting their self in the other, and that is exactly what they are doing. Such a person not only speaks *to* us but *for* us, and we for them. Keep this in mind when you are looking for a spiritual teacher, whether in book or bodily form. When you find a spiritual teacher who speaks for you, voicing what you inwardly know to be true, you have found one of your teachers.

THE NEW SCIENCES

Quantum science is now showing us a creation that is seamless, meaning everything is connected. The relatively recent theories of entanglement and non local cause reveal we don't even need to be near each other to affect and be effected by each other. Scientists have evidence that this is so but do not yet know HOW this is so.

At the quantum level, when it comes to sub-atomic particles, there are no solid boundaries between any of the forms that make up our experience. People, objects, mountains, rivers, galaxies, and even our thought forms and feelings are all interconnected. Like clouds of invisible energy, we and everything all rub up against each other, meld into each other, affect each other. All affects all, whether we consciously realize it yet or not.

One cell in your stomach can cause other cells in your stomach to be affected in some way. Pollution in one country can affect weather conditions in another. When a person coughs in Germany, it may contribute to a collection of germs that cause a breakout of head colds in Canada.

When a person dies of starvation, for example, in some small measure, all experience the pain and sadness. Equally, when one person becomes more conscious, it helps to raise the consciousness of others.

ONENESS THROUGH DIVERSITY, NOT SAMENESS

We create through the diversity of our unique essence within our

Oneness. Many of us have mistaken our Oneness with sameness. Just like every snowflake is unique but made up of the same substance, we, as consciousness itself, are unique aspects of the whole of creation. Our true Self is infinitely diverse, and you and I are its expressions. We will always carry with us the uniqueness of our individual expression of creation as it changes and evolves, just like we observe during our lifetime that we grow and change in our body and in our beliefs and level of awareness.

A LEAP INTO GLOBAL ONENESS

So often our way of approaching life is ego-driven. When we identify with ego as if it were who we really are, we simply can't see our Oneness with the rest of our species, let alone our Oneness with the whole of creation. We don't recognize that we all come from the same Source that permeates the entire cosmos. It's the Oneness that science is now unveiling and that we are, through our communication technologies, now catching a glimpse of on a worldwide scale. Even though the increased contact we have with each other through the modern communication technologies is up to this point mostly at a surface level and lacks deep connection, the stage has been set.

The urgency of shifting from a collective egoic mentality of "me" to one of "we" is evident when we look at some of humanity's current challenges, such as global warming, the threat of large-scale pandemics, terrorism, and nuclear proliferation. These reach beyond any sectarian or national boundaries, prompting the need for co-operation among individuals, communities, nations, and world leaders. Our interdependence can no longer be denied. Other-interest *is* self-interest. Global-interest *is* national-interest.

Life speaks to us frequently of our Oneness, but do we have eyes, the awareness to see this evidence? Once we become mindful of something in our life, we begin to see frequent evidence of it. Take the newly pregnant woman who then sees other pregnant women almost everywhere, amazed she never noticed so many before; or the man who buys a new car and now notices so many of the same car on the roads. This is because awareness, through personal experience, tends to draw to us repeated evidence of what we have now become aware of. So, let's pay attention to the evidence of Oneness in our lives and note the increasing number of incidents that attest to this. No matter how much we talk about the Oneness of the true Self, it is only when we come to *experience* the evidence of Oneness that it is not a concept but a reality for us. *A Course in Miracles* states: "A universal theology is impossible, but a universal experience is not only possible but necessary." [2]

PRACTICE

Take time to note how similar you are to others, whether they be family members, work associates, or people you meet for a short time and on a casual basis. Once you notice the similarity between you and others, do you feel a stronger connection to them?

PRACTICE

Take note of times when you unexpectedly met with another person, when there seemed no evident way, cause, or reason to meet them. Were you able to discern a reason for your surprisingly connecting with them?

13

THE WORLD NEEDS YOUR SERVICE

"I slept and I dreamed that life was all joy.
I woke and I saw that life is all service.
I served and I saw that service is joy."

Kahil Gibran

ANYONE CAN SERVE

You don't have to have a lot of money, a college degree or be young to serve. All you need is love in your heart that you want to extend to your brothers and sisters by taking some action, however small, with the intent to assist them in some way.

Many of those who meditate regularly have a strong desire to be of service to others — perhaps because through meditation one comes to sense their Oneness with all that lives. Whether you meditate or not, most people who develop the spiritual dimension of their life want to work with purpose, have meaning in their life, know that they are contributing to making the lives of those they love and humanity as a whole better in whatever way they see "better" being.

St. Hildegard of Bingen, who twice took to her bed in a state of depression, got herself out of it by telling herself, "I must be useful." In looking at the lives of Dr. David Hawkins, Barry Long, and Joel S. Goldsmith, who are now deceased, and Eckhart Tolle still living - all who awoke to their true nature when in the body - lived thereafter being of service to humanity.

I am so often asked, "What can I do to be of service? I want to have a larger purpose to my life." My immediate response is always the same: Ask yourself, "How best may I be of service at this time?" Ask this with heartfelt sincerity and the wisdom within you will answer. The answer may not come immediately but in stages. Stay alert to why and how Life, our greatest teacher, is directing you.

In Victor Frankl's classic *Man's Search for Meaning*, he tells us that a man who has a *why* to live can bear with any *how*. When a prisoner in both Auschwitz and Dachau, Frankl became a keen observer of his fellow inmates. Over time, he noticed that it was not necessarily those physically stronger or with no apparent physical illness who survived. He watched these die in the same numbers as the weak and sickly. He pondered why this was so. In time, Frankl became aware of the answer. A prisoner who had something to live for: a wife, a family, a book to write or finish, a meaningful profession to resume, and so forth were the most likely to survive because they had a purpose for living. Other prisoners who saw no one to return to and nothing else that was meaningful in their lives yet to do or achieve were the first to die. They lacked a reason to continue suffering through their then horrific life and gave up the will to live.

After surviving the holocaust, Frankl became the Founder of Logo-therapy, "Logos" being the Latin word for "meaning" and Logo-therapy a form of existential analysis.

Hence, Frankl stresses it *is up to us* to give our lives meaning, purpose. But in the throes of devastation, deep pain and debilitating loss, it is hard to do this. That's when we often need to turn to a therapist.

Frankl, a neurologist and psychiatrist, wrote of his clinical practice. He tells of one case when a renowned and successful man came to him in complete emotional collapse. He could not shake the emotional pain, lethargy and ennui following the loss of his beloved wife. He was rendered paralyzed in terms of negotiating his way in the world and continuing his work. Frankl spent only one session with this man. He asked him, "What would your wife be feeling now if you had died first?" The man paused, went inward, then responded, "Well, she would be going through what I am now." It didn't take the man more than a moment to find meaning in his suffering. He saw himself as suffering in her stead. He recovered quickly and went back into the world and to his work.

Similarly, it is up to us to infuse our life with a sense of meaning. Service gives meaning to our lives, but our service purpose doesn't come from "out there". It is never imposed upon us.

THE IMPACT OF YOUR SERVICE CANNOT BE MEASURED

Your service mission does not have to be huge or even noticeable to others. I was told of a woman named Grace who went off to work early each morning with a smile on her face and a bounce in her walk. Her next-door neighbor observed this daily and one day got up the boldness to meet her as she left her house and asked, "What kind of work do you do? You must really love it."

"Oh, I do." responded Grace. "I help prevent the spread of infectious diseases."

"Really?" responded her neighbor. "How do you do that?"

"I work in a factory that makes rubber gloves for hospitals and other medical workers and caretakers."

Closer to home - literally - there was a homeless person who nightly, as he scoured through the back lanes, collected things he perceived could be of value to others. Instead of just leaving them there, he took them to an empty corner lot where a gas station once was but due to safety reasons needed to be free of any other use for the government's prescribed number of years. Surrounding the out-of-bounds site was a wire fence that provided a perfect hanger-like structure for the homeless man to show his "treasures", which he invited others to pick-up if they needed them. Over time, others brought things. Used furniture, older bikes, and so forth were positioned in front of the fence. Almost-new clothing was hung on it. This anonymous man, while still living, had been a true inspiration to our community to give to others what we have in surplus.

FINDING YOUR SERVICE PURPOSE

When do you become aware of your service purpose? Before you incarnate? In the womb? After a near fatal illness, during a

THE WORLD NEEDS YOUR SERVICE

moment of crisis, after a huge aha experience? It will be different for everyone. It may become evident early or later in your life.

I know of a person who knew that her purpose in life was to be a good mother. Through hard work and unwavering willpower, while also living with an abusive husband and in semi-poverty, she brought up eight children. They were not only given whatever "bread" she could give them but also the "honey" of being taught how to live a spiritual life.

The form of your service may come into your awareness suddenly one day as it did with Mother Teresa.

On her way back from a spiritual retreat, Mother Teresa was on a bus that travelled through what was then called Calcutta. Previous to this, she led quite a remote life, isolated from the masses in India. The story goes that on that day, she took it upon herself to do some exploring. Mother was horrified at the poverty, sickness, and homelessness she saw. On her way back home, as she sat on the bus, her heart ached for the disadvantaged people she saw. With great anguish she knew how huge and many the problems were. Knowing this, she asked herself, "But what can I do, just one person?" This question led her into stillness out of which came her answer. "You can try to be with as many dying people as you can so they don't have to die alone." We know the rest of the story and how her service actions attracted a whole order of other women, the Sisters of Charity, and how she influenced all of us to be actively of service to the less fortunate.

Once you have identified your service purpose that is suitable and viable in your current life circumstances and act on it, you will likely take a wonderful ride. The ride will be different for each of us and different at various life stages. Following are some predictable things that may occur.

If you are not already doing so, you will be drawn into a regular spiritual practice. You will start to crave times of stillness. And in that stillness, you will become acquainted with that guiding voice within you. As you continue in service, your ego will start to weaken. As this occurs, love will trump fear in your life. You will forget about having to do things perfectly and in letting that need based on fear go will do things better than you possibly expected – and with ease. You will be guided and make clear decisions because your service intent is uncompromisingly clear.

Even though your commitment to be of service is heart-driven, your service work, especially when young or in the early stages, may take some time to be devoid of ego. That is to be expected.

As you continue in noble service, predictably your service influence will grow. There is an extensive passage in I Chronicles 4:10. In this passage, a long list of names is given of those who were beloved and blessed by God. The list goes on – name after name – until it comes to Jabez. Then there is a noticeable shift. It not only cites his name, but also goes into more detail. It cites his prayer to God.

> "And Jabez called on the God of Israel saying,
> 'Oh, that You would bless me indeed,
> and enlarge my territory,
> that Your hand would be with me,
> and that You would keep me from evil,
> that I may not cause pain!'

So God granted him what he requested."

Why? Because Jabez prayed a perfect prayer for wanting to be of service. When Jabez refers to enlarging his territory, he means his service territory, his service influence.

What a powerful prayer for those who want to be of service to say daily.

Be aware that you will be challenged and tested along the way – and usually just before you are about to take a leap in your service work so your "territory" can expand. Do you still come from a pure selfless service intent or has ego crept back in? One needs to be vigilant, as the dark does not want to support the light. Your vigilance will be known by your ongoing and stepped up spiritual practices.

You will have to make decisions, of course, but you will make them with greater ease and clarity knowing that although you have to have a leg in both worlds—the physical world and the spiritual—it is the spiritual leg you must always lean upon for direction.

It is important to remember that you don't need to do anything alone. You are free to call upon the support from your seen helpers such as your family, friends, spiritual teachers. Also, call for help from the unseen realms such as your ancestors, your awakened Self, the angelic realm, the realm of the Ascended Masters. Ask for help and they will answer your call. Why? Because the Spiritual Law of Oneness ensures that they are already part of your One Self.

Rest in the knowing that as an individual you need do very little –

other than hold to your service intent, show up, and take the next step as you feel inwardly guided to take. As you lovingly wield your intention and attention, Life will bring you everything you need to continue in your service work. You will sometimes feel like you are being carried, buoyed like an eagle that can make a swooping turn by a slight movement of wing.

You may experience what seems like a charmed life. Synchronicities and serendipitous events may abound. Skills and intuition will likely rapidly increase. Blessings in all forms may flow into your life – not because you sought them but as the "fruits" of your service work. When you serve others, Life cannot but give back to you blessings in abundance. Why? Because when you come from service to humanity, you come from love for humanity. As *A Course in Miracles* tells us, miracles are a product, an outcome of expressed love.

We also need to be alerted that our life will still be challenging because we will be continuously pushed to grow in our service work in order to come from a higher level of compassion, love, and consciousness. As already mentioned, we are here in our human form in this lifetime to do just that—to grow in consciousness. Out of love, Life will give us these challenges to do so.

PRACTICE
With little deliberation, write your life line to date. What do you see that may indicate your inclination to a particular kind of service work?

PRACTICE
Next, go to Appendix B at the back of the book and read the

questions there. Give attention to each question, then revisit what you recently wrote for your life line. What would you now add to or write about your life line? Do these additions help you see more clearly where and how you are now inclined and able to be of service?

14

WHAT DOES COMING FROM HIGHER CONSCIOUSNESS "LOOK LIKE"?

"The most telling and profound way of describing the evolution of the universe would undoubtedly be to trace the evolution of love."

Pierre Teilhard de Chardin

TRUE WEALTH

We each have within our hearts the means to create lives that exude true richness, since love is the only real treasure of value. We are deluded if we think that any artificial form of exchange such as money, gold, precious stones, property, or valuable objects can produce anything of *real* value. The only real treasures are those we acquire through loving.

Extending love pays abundant dividends. It is a universally desired "commodity". Always in demand, its value never deteriorates. Neither can we exhaust our supply of love because we *are* love.

Imagine the kind of world we would create if we all strove to be rich in love and measured our self-worth accordingly. Unless we are mentally challenged in any way, we all have equal ability to express the love that we are and thereby would end our spiritual poverty.

LIVING FROM THE HEART

The more you meditate, the more you become aware of your true nature. And along with that comes an increasing capacity to love yourself and desire to extend love to others by your thoughts, words, actions, and prayers. As you continue in your regular spiritual practices, including meditation, one day you will likely find yourself thinking more of the welfare of "others". There is a shift of primary focus on "me" to an increased focus on "we". Once you focus on the "we", your focus and felt connection with others naturally become stronger.

EXTENDING LOVING KINDNESS

METTA PRAYER

The Buddha recommended to his disciples that they practice Metta Prayer, which is a prayer of good will and loving kindness toward yourself and others. Almost always, I end a workshop or presentation with a Metta Prayer. Following is one I am deeply drawn to.

> May I be at peace.
> May my heart remain open.
> May I awaken to the light of my own true nature.
> May I be healed.
> May I be a source of healing for all beings.

Notice the prayer uses the pronoun "I". We first have to extend love to ourselves and thereby become more loving human beings. As we do this, our Metta Prayers become more powerful.

If you want to adopt the practice of saying this Metta Prayer, start by saying it for yourself. Then say it for someone who is very close to you and you love. Next for someone in your life for whom you have neutral feelings. Follow this by saying it for someone you dislike or even go so far as to think of as an enemy.

Then you can move from "you" to "they" and say it for a group, such as your family, those in prison, those without homes to live in, single parents, those grieving a loved one, and many others.

These people do not need to know about your praying for them or be open to receiving this prayer at their end. This is about you growing your capacity to love through Metta Prayer. Over time, your heart will open and soften to even those you dislike. This may result in an evident positive change in your relationship with them or not. This is not important. Love sincerely extended to another always brings positive effects, at least for the one extending the prayer.

Finally, you can extend the prayer to include all of humanity, Mother Earth, all sentient creatures and life forms.

In one workshop, when I took the participants through the complete sequence above, one woman said, "How can I take all of humanity into my heart?" Another quickly responded, "Of course you can." Thinking you cannot open your heart to embrace all of humanity comes from believing our capacity to take others into our heart is limited. The power of the heart has no boundaries, its capacity to extend is never-ending.

PRACTICE
Write your own heartfelt Metta Prayer and say it daily or as often as you are drawn to do so—first for yourself, then for others.

EXPRESSING YOUR TRUE NATURE

If you want to start experiencing your true nature, don't go to the past to figure out how to live in the present. When you have grown in consciousness, the past holds only a limited story of yourself. Thinking back to the past, looking to it for guidance, serves only to lock you into your story, closing the door to your true Self, which is experienced only in the present.

You can never express your true Self and all of its attributes such as love, joy, and peace in the past. If it is important for your spiritual evolution to remember something from the past, it will come to you in the present, at the moment you need it. Sometimes this happens when you need to heal emotional wounds from the past that still need healing.

If you want to experience your true nature, don't escape to the future either, as the future is nothing but wishful thinking or fearful projection, both still based on your past.

I have had the privilege of working with two enlightened authors. In both instances, their enlightenment came through a sudden experience of breaking identity with the ego. Once the false self fell away, their true Self naturally emerged.

Suddenly becoming enlightened is not the experience for most of us. We can either wait for this rare occurrence to happen to us too, or we can shake ourselves awake by expressing the love we already are.

How can I recognize that I am only love?

By extending love to all, at all times. It is only by giving love that you come to the realization that you are the love you are giving.

As you practice being loving, likely you will find yourself becoming more buoyant and feeling more "alive", because you cannot extend the love that you are without this healing and elevating energy coming back to you. When it does, it reminds you that you can't really give love away because you are the source of the love you give.

Everything simply works better when we live from our true Self. As we extend love, our body produces more endorphins that bring about a heightened sense of well-being. As we continue to practice living from our true nature, it feels so good to be who we truly are that we no longer want to do anything to diminish this experience. Once we start living from our true nature, any lapse that takes us back to the uncomfortable false egoic self with its fear-driven behavior only serves to underscore that we are not *that*.

How would we love if we were not impeded by the ego? Our true Self exudes love and holds only gratitude for opportunities to extend it. There will be differences in the way the various attributes of our true Self are expressed through us because some of us are more enthusiastic; some of us more quietly confident; some of us more ebullient in nature and others more serene.

Unconditional love, ah how rare it is. The hallmark of unconditional love is that it is devoid of fear. In the absence of fear, there is nothing to impede the flow of our love. This is why love can only be extended by our true Self, not the egoic self that grew out of and is sustained by fear. It is also why many spiritual teachers tell us to resist nothing and to surrender to what is. In order to do this, we need to drop fear. By doing so, we open the way for our love to flow into all our experiences and beyond us into our world.

Unconditional love has no choice but to extend itself. It is universally inclusive. It doesn't require anything of the objects of its love. Since it goes beyond personal love, it takes nothing personally and therefore cannot be slighted. Such love is not limited by any boundaries. It is never disturbed because it sees only the reality of love in all persons and situations, although this love is masked at times, and sometimes heavily so. It is without judgment and doesn't need to wait until someone is "perfect" before it extends love to them. It unconditionally accepts all—all people and all situations as they are right now.

At the visceral level, when we love unconditionally, there is a softening of our perceptions and a softening of the way we experience being in the body.

A test of whether your love is pure is to ask if there is any fear in your love: fear of betrayal, fear of the other leaving you, fear of the other not acting or being what you want them to do or be. Ask yourself: "When I love my spouse or partner, is this love free of fear? When I love my children, is my love given without fear of them turning out in a certain way? Of not living up to my expectations?" Of course parents have concern about their children's welfare and safety, but responsible concern followed by caring action is not fear. Regarding the first question, you might answer, "There is no fear in my love for my spouse, but I do fear their dying."

That's anticipatory grief and can be expected as long as we are in the body and our love for someone includes their form. When a loved one dies, only the body dies. Their essence, their Being continues to exist. Still we miss the form: the warm smile, the look from their eyes, their touch, their sense of humor, their companionship, and so on. Anticipatory grief regarding someone we love dearly is anticipating the personal pain we will experience once the form goes, since love always wants to be fully connected in all ways to the beloved. Anticipatory grief is one of the occasions when we experience fear and love at the same time, but fear is the predominant factor.

Why is fear the more dominant emotion? Because the person is *anticipating* and therefore not in the present moment. If they came back to what is at the time, they would just be with their loved one extending love.

Many of us would say that we love God, although many of us have been brought up to fear God. How can one fear that which is only Love? To equate fear with God is an oxymoron, yet it is one many of us have lived with for a time. Fear by its very nature leads to the illusion so many of us hold that we are separate from God. We cut ourselves off from the realization of our true nature because of this fear. However, we can never cut ourselves off from our Divine Source.

Do you love your life? Many have a love-fear relationship with their lives. Their enjoyment of life is undercut by a deep distrust—a sense that the proverbial "other shoe" is about to drop.

A woman got into an elevator and a maintenance man with a bucket entered along with her. He immediately struck up a conversation by asking, "How are you today?"

"I'm just wonderful!" she enthused.

"Oh, I'd never say that," the maintenance man responded. "I'd be afraid that if I let myself feel that good, I'd have to pay for it later. I prefer to stay in the groove."

What a pity! This man was cutting himself off from the joy of life because of his belief that life can't be trusted to bring him amazingly good things.

The maintenance man isn't alone in feeling a distrust of life. Have you ever noticed that whenever a person says they feel wonderful and really means it, people look at them like they must be fibbing. Why? Because such people have never allowed themselves to experience with abandonment the joy of living.

When we don't believe that love is the basis of everything, we don't trust life to be absolutely supportive, benign, and giving to us; therefore, we fear life, at least to a degree. The energy of fear is highly creative. That is why if we continuously dwell on what we fear, we are likely to have what we fear manifest in our lives. People also tend to be afraid of another's pain. When we run from being with others in their pain, we are not coming from love but from fear of vicariously experiencing the pain of the other or fear that such misfortune could also happen to us. Can we as parents claim to love our children in a way that we don't run from or enter into fear when they experience acute pain in their lives? Can we trust in their inner wisdom and the wisdom of Life itself, even when they go against our wishes or stray from our personal values?

LOVE HAS MANY FORMS OF EXPRESSION

Love is not always expressed in a soft and warm manner. Sometimes it is boldly expressed and may initially be experienced as aggressive.

A Zen story illustrates this beautifully. After his three students had a long period of intense study and practices, the Zen master suggested they go into town for a break, to shop and enjoy the sights of the marketplace. The students responded with delight to this suggestion and quickly headed off. Since the market was a distance away, they decided to take a rickshaw. Upon climbing into the rickshaw, the female student was attacked by a thief who wrestled with her for her purse. That evening after supper, the Zen master asked his students how they enjoyed their day in town. The female student told of how her purse was stolen from her. The master listened with great attention. When the girl had concluded the story, the master said, "Oh, my dear, why didn't you, *with the most loving kindness in your heart*, hit the thief over the head with your umbrella to stop him?"

The Zen master was teaching his students that we need to go to our heart first to assess the most appropriate, most loving response, then take action. A plea of, "Please don't steal my purse," would have fallen on deaf ears, as would saying, "Please don't take this. It contains the only money I have to buy a present for my master."

The Zen master knew that this situation called for a sharp physical rebuke—a purposeful but hard knock to stop the thief. Such a response is an act of love—not because it might save the purse to buy the present for the master, but because it might cause the thief to "listen up" in the only way he could at his level of consciousness at the time.

You may ask HOW can I remain concerned about the well-being of someone who is about to attack me? The preceding Zen story gives us a clue. Suppose a burglar breaks into your house. What do you do? You try to stop him. It's your home, and he shouldn't have broken in. In defending yourself, however, try to do so "with the most loving kindness in your heart", and if you can't do that, come from a place of emotional neutrality. If you don't react with fear-evoked anger, your "Inner Knower" will guide you in what is best to do in the situation. And by not being overtaken by fear, you will predictably come from inner calmness, taking alert action and thereby minimizing the negative repercussions for both yourself and the burglar.

It is up to us to discern how to most appropriately express our love in different situations. This means being open to the still small voice of our Inner Knower to guide us. Sometimes words or actions will not be called for, just a silent blessing of the person or situation, or visualizing them being surrounded by healing white light.

COMPASSION TRUMPS SYMPATHY

Recall the occasion on which Mother Teresa found a newborn infant in a Calcutta gutter. There was no pity in her eyes as she gazed at this infant, only adoring love flowing from the recognition of the perfect being she was holding in the palm of her hand. Mother Teresa was able to move from human sympathy to compassion. She looked at the tiny babe with eyes filled with compassion, and the babe responded from the life incarnate in it.

When we come from human sympathy, there is a separation between the other and our Self. Compassion emerges from our inner awareness of Oneness.

When it comes to nations attacking each other, the tendency is to teach armed forces to objectify the "enemy". But to defend ourselves, we don't need to turn others into inhuman objects. When we do this, we cannot see our One Self and can more easily deny the other person's value and thus act against them without conscience. Just as with the burglar, we can do what needs to be done from the most loving place in our heart. We take prudent defensive action, but we don't buy into and mimic back the hateful spirit from which the military "enemy" may come.

In the martial arts, a contestant respects their opponent. This respect is an important aspect of achieving emotional balance. Contestants know that they must remain emotionally neutral by honoring their opponent as an equal if they are to have the inner balance that allows their intense strength to come through.

Can we consider the benefit of honoring our "enemy" as being part of our One Self when in self-defense or defense of any nation? Is this a way one can emerge from such conflict in a healthy emotional and spiritual state?

Can we consider what healing power would be released if we could love our enemy? By doing good to those who do us harm? What a challenge, but also what an opportunity to take a huge step to higher consciousness.

Do we always feel peaceful and warm when we love unconditionally? No. But to not run from pain - either in ourselves or in others - but to embrace it, is an act of supreme love. It is perhaps during such times, when the heart physically seems to burn and break open with pain, that our love is most redemptive. We stand resolute in the pain, resisting nothing—not even focusing on hope that it will end. Our only purpose becomes to face the sadness, disaster, or tragedy and fully surrender to it.

If you sit with your emotional pain and let it be, feeling fully the energy of this state, you will discover that there is something beneath it. Emotional pain that is accepted, then embraced, begins to soften and break up. As it does so, a new state emerges that is still and peaceful. If you run from your pain, doing anything you can to avoid feeling it, you prevent yourself from experiencing the reality of peace underneath it.

Anyone who has fully surrendered themselves to grieving the loss of a loved one, including a beloved pet, will tell you that they had to feel the deep and excruciating pain of loss before they could come to the awareness that they could never really lose the other, that they will always be connected with them, that their authentic love between them endures and goes on forever.

When we cannot accept, we create from a state of non-acceptance. If we run from our fear, we create out of fear. If we run from our pain, we create out of pain. Instead of resisting or running, if we accept these states, even embrace them, we are able to let go of the fear-based conditioned past from which they emanate. We can then heal and start anew.

SPIRITUAL INTEGRITY

We want to do worthwhile things so that we have a positive influence in the world. Mahatma Gandhi emphasized putting being and doing in the correct order. One of his most quoted sayings is, "First *be* the truth you want to see in others."

At one point in his life, Gandhi agreed to set aside certain times during the week when he would receive people. On one such occasion, a woman and her son were brought to him. The woman was distressed and explained to Gandhi that her son was making himself sick by eating too much candy. No matter what she said or what discipline she applied, her son continued to eat abundant amounts of sweets. "Mahatma, Mahatma, please tell him not to eat sweets," she pleaded. "He will listen to you. Please, Mahatma, please."

Gandhi looked at the boy, then back at the mother, then once again at the boy. Turning back to the mother, he responded, "Please come back with your son in three days."

The mother left with her son and both returned at the appointed time. When they were ushered in to see him, Gandhi stood up to greet them, then walked straight to within a few feet of the boy. To emphasize his words, Gandhi raised his right hand and pointed his index finger at the boy, then in a calm but serious voice said, "Don't eat sweets." The mother quickly piped up. "What, Mahatma? That is all you have to say? Why didn't you tell my son this three days ago?"

Without hesitation Gandhi answered, "Because three days ago, I was still eating sweets."

Gandhi was showing us that to be a teacher of spiritual truth, we first need to embody the teaching. In other words, we *are* the teaching. We have to be people of integrity who embody what we teach; otherwise, we will be ineffective. Gandhi knew that his instruction not to eat sweets would fall on deaf ears unless he was already living this himself. We too need to know that the power we have to effect positive change and healing in our world comes from practicing before we teach.

This is why the content of some spiritual books has real transformative power, whereas others do not. Transformative books emerge from the authentic state of Being they are trying to bring to the awareness of their readers. As such, a transference takes place as the writer's state of Being is carried through the words and extended to the reader, thereby awakening in the reader, to some degree, this state within them as well.

As shared earlier, Presence is not only powerful, it is magnetic, evoking the Presence in others, whether they are already conscious of their inner Presence or not.

To bring peace into a situation, we first have to be at peace ourselves. We must embody the qualities of tolerance, non-judgment, acceptance, and respect that we want to see in the world. For example, to foster the dissolution of terrorism, we first need to stop our own attack thoughts and strategies—in all their varied forms of intensity from subtle to fierce.

BLESSING IS A POWERFUL ACT

On a trip from Vancouver, Canada, to Los Angeles, I had to pass through U.S. Customs. It wasn't busy that morning, so no one was marshaling us into particular lines. Since I could choose whichever customs officer I wanted to go to, I scanned their faces, and one caught my eye. His expression was warm, his countenance inviting.

"You marked the purpose of your trip as both personal and business," he said.

"Yes, I'm speaking at a church in Orange County," I explained. "I am a publisher and the congregation has read a number of the books we have published. Given the success story of my small publishing house and our publishing mission, they wanted to hear what I had to say."

"What areas do you publish in?" the officer asked. "Spirituality and personal development," I replied.

"Spirituality!" he exclaimed. "That's what we need. You know, I am not really a customs officer. I am an undercover "blesser". Working as a customs officer is a way to meet people. If I didn't meet you, how could I bless you?" He nodded at a group of people who entered at that moment. "Look at all these people. Look at how many I get to bless."

"You don't need my talk!" I responded. "But I am sure going to tell my audience about you."

"Have a wonderful trip," he said with a smile.

This was a United States customs officer! Instead of feeling under suspicion or intimidated, I was welcomed with warmth. This officer left me with an awareness of the goodness to be found in the most unexpected people and places.

Such a lovely story, yet there is something the U.S. customs officer couldn't do on the job that we can to make our blessing of others even more powerful. That is to bless someone out loud using their name. There is more power in the spoken word. Bless others out loud when you are alone or with them. Ask others to bless you out loud. When you bless, you extend loving intentions to the one you are blessing.

Parents have the opportunity to bless their children out loud every day, and better yet, several times a day. At home we can bless our food out loud. How many of us have gotten away from this positive practice?

When in a public restaurant we refrain from blessing out loud since we don't want to attract attention or make others who are not so inclined uncomfortable. I know of a restaurant founded on spiritual principles and sincere service. Those who are in the kitchen gather every morning and bless the food they will be using to prepare the meals for the day. One can literally *feel* a beautiful energy when eating there. And the food is beyond delicious.

Just as courtesy can be the beginning of charity, so also blessing others can be the beginning of unconditional love. When we genuinely bless others, the love we extend is egoless. We don't want something from the other; we want only good things for them.

Through the work of Masaru Emoto and scientists Kurt Wuthrich, Nobel Prize Winner from Switzerland, Martin Chaplin, Vladamir Voyekov, as well as other scientists from countries around the world such as Russia, Switzerland, Israel, Great Britain, USA, Argentina, China, we have come to understand the phenomenal importance and properties of water. [1]

According to scientists who have studied water, water has memory. It feels and responds to our thoughts and emotions. It remembers everything it takes in around it. Anything or anyone coming near it leaves its trace on it. There is a chemical component to water, that being H_2O. Even more importantly, water has a *structural* component. We can change the molecular structure of water by our thoughts, words, emotions. Human presence and emotion have the strongest influence on water. Talking to or thinking about water in positive ways has a beneficial effect on it, meaning it increases its life-giving energy. Saying out loud or internally words like "I love you. You are beautiful. I thank you. I bless you" can change the molecules from misshapen, murky water configurations to beautiful and symmetrical hexagonal crystal-like formations. Expressed love increases the benefit of water. Negative thoughts and emotions do just the opposite. The greatest positive effect or change we can make upon water is when we feel and speak emotions of love and gratitude.

The Japanese Scientist Masaru Emoto experimented with 3 glasses of rice that he poured water over. Every day for a month he

approached the glasses of rice. To one glass he said, "Thank you."
To another glass of rice he said, "You are an idiot." He ignored the
third glass. The result? After a month the glass that was shown
appreciation had fermented. The rice that was told it was an idiot
turned black. The third glass that was ignored began to rot.[2]

There are other interesting documented incidents to attest to how
water absorbs and is affected by our thoughts and emotions. For
example, in 1956 a group of scientists gathered at a secret military
laboratory in South East Asia to discuss and work on developing
germ warfare. At one such protracted meeting, all of the members
in the group got sick, showing symptoms of severe food poisoning.
They were rushed to the hospital. Their illness wasn't caused by
food poisoning, since all they had was the water from the carafe on
the desk they sat around. Their toxic and threatening conversation
so affected the water they drank that it became harmful to their
health. [3]

Going all the way back to 1472, according to the chronicles of the
time, an Abbott was imprisoned because he was believed to have
poisoned a royal woman. In prison he was given only a crust of
bread and polluted water to drink each day. The Abbott gave
thanksgiving and recited a prayer over the bread and putrid water.
The result? He improved in health. However, this worked against
him because then it was thought it was proof he was possessed. [4]

If extending love to water by blessing it can have such a dramatic
and positive effect, how healing it must be when we bless each
other, since the human body is made up of approximately 70-90%
water, depending on age. The brain is made up of approximately
80% water. Bless your brain and intend it to have only positive

thoughts.

You don't have to be a priest or deemed a holy person to bless water and make it life-giving. We can all bless our water. And don't forget Mother Earth. She is made up of so much water. We love Mother Earth, but we have to love her more.

Bless and thereby extend the good. Bless your enemy, bless your pet, bless the mail carrier, bless your plants and the water you give them, bless all who enter your home. Create a plaque stating your house blessings and put it at your entrance. Then, hold to the intent that everyone who enters your home will receive these blessings when they enter and take them with them when they leave.

THE POWER OF NOBLE INTENTION

In 1996, I shared with one of my business colleagues that I wanted to deepen my spirituality. It so happened that he had just met a man who had arrived from England a few weeks earlier who was said to be a spiritual teacher. "I'll ask if he would be open to leading sessions in your office," he said.

A week later, at the end of the workday, our office door opened and in walked a gentle, unassuming man who was introduced to me as Eckhart Tolle. Within a couple of weeks, I recognized what a profound and timely teacher he was, especially for the West. Each week Eckhart led us deeper into stillness and spiritual awareness.

As time passed, I learned that Eckhart was writing a book, and in due course he asked me to be his publisher. I had never published a book before, but I felt compelled to make *The Power of Now* available to the world. We joined in Oneness, setting our intention, without any expectations, without any sense of whether a handful of people or millions would read it. The book came out in 1998, defying publishing norms as it spread quickly by word of mouth, without advertising. To date it has sold over 6 million copies in North America alone, almost 8 million in the English language, and is available in 45 languages. It was the form born of our joining in Oneness with a common noble intention.

Intention is causative. To intend is requisite to creating. It precedes visualization. Often people feel that if they visualize something, they are creating it. But visualization is only a tool, not the creative source. The same is true of prayer, whether it is uttered verbally or silently. Indeed, both visualization and prayer are fostered by and flow *from* intent.

Intent is more formless than visualization and prayer and therefore carries a more refined and powerful creative energy.

Intent is an expression of faith. It is something that is strongly held but not controlled by will, mental effort, or manipulation. Although intent holds to an end state, this end state is not specific in detail and has its own characteristic feeling signature.

Take the example of holding to the intent of having a healthy relationship with your partner. You make no assumptions as to *how* the healthy relationship will be achieved. Intent does not prescribe what is necessary for your relationship to be healthy. As you hold to your intent, the relationship just naturally becomes healthier, in the most appropriate ways. You may be quite surprised by what follows. For example, you may find yourself speaking more openly, honestly, and spontaneously to your partner, without having planned to do so. You may find yourself with a new awareness of your partner's challenges, which leads to a deeper understanding and level of caring in your relationship. You may find more time for each other. And even if you don't, the time you spend together may result in your becoming more in tune and deeply devoted to each other.

When you hold to an intention, it does not mean that you are passive. On the contrary, holding to your intent requires an investment of energy. This energy may feel different to you at first. Although there is a generalized thought component to intent, it is not mental energy that is generative but heart-felt energy. Whatever needs to be done through or by you will become evident. The guidance you require will often be given at the precise moment you need it. When the spiritual power of your noble intention is unleashed, watch what happens! This is when you experience synchronicities, delightful "accidents", coincidences, and what may be called "miracles". There is no grand announcement or fanfare, just amazing results.

EGO-BASED INTENTION

While all intention is powerful, intention can arise from two different sources. The effect in each case is also quite different. Intention can be ego-based. This often involves a desire for status, prestige, power, or wealth. Your intentions are wrapped up with yourself, so they tend to be narcissistic. It's all about you—your comfort, security, and success.

Ego-based intention, no matter how positive it may appear, is actually rooted in the negative emotion of fear. Driven by a sense of personal lack, it is need-based. When intention springs from your feelings of inadequacy, you have a need to prove something to yourself and more often to others.

When intention is based in ego, you may accomplish a great deal. The more intensely you feel you have to acquire or achieve something, the more likely you are to hone in on your intention in a powerful way. But intention that is ego-based bears the hallmark of a voracious vacuum sucking into itself. Whenever intention emanates from an egoic state of mind, the good it can achieve is restricted by the boundaries of self-interest.

NOBLE INTENTION

Intention can also be what I call "noble". Whether or not an intent is noble is determined by the motivation behind it. If an intent is noble, it will not be based on egoic need and gratification.

Instead of being motivated primarily by money, fame, status, or power, noble intention is love-based and flows from your heart. You come from a higher consciousness, and your intentions simply well up from the goodness within you. It is a noble intention primarily because it concerns your own personal and spiritual growth or the betterment of others. Your focus is on the possibilities for blessing the world, not on personal gain.

When you hold to a noble intention, you are coming from the core of your Being, which is love. Your intention, the initial stage of creativity, is an extension of your true Self. Because its accomplishments are the outcomes of love, they bring about lasting good for you and for all concerned.

When you come from noble intent, your true Self will withhold nothing. This is because it is safe to shower you with all good things, since you will not misuse these things in service to the ego. Because your motivation is not money, you will not be attached to financial abundance if it comes to you. You can fully and joyfully appreciate the financial abundance, but you will not fear losing it. Although abundance is not the motivation of your intent, it comes back to you in all forms as the "fruits" of it.

Prestige may come with your success. But because it wasn't sought after, you will remain free of ego and not be attached to your higher profile. You will have no egoic need to hold on to it. You will enjoy the higher personal profile, not as a matter of self-importance, but because of the doors it opens to you for further avenues of service.

When you take the power of intention and make it noble by holding it for your spiritual growth, the good of another, or humanity in general, you ignite it with spiritual rocket fuel. Being causative, such an intention can only bring about positive results. Because it is without ego, expect quicker manifestation, since ego impedes progress with fear-based worry, doubt, hesitation, and vacillation.

Since what you are doing is not in service of the ego, the result cannot be anything but a blessing to others. And when others are blessed, the one who holds the intention is also blessed. It is a spiritual law that when we love, we are loved.

It is up to each of us to determine if we want to invest our actions with a higher purpose. For example, you can produce a movie in order to become famous or wealthy, or you can do the same from noble intent, seeking only to elevate the consciousness of viewers. Both require intent, but one is ego-based and the other noble.

LIVE INTENTIONALLY EVERY DAY

The riches of noble intent are always available for harvesting, no matter what your particular walk of life.

Suppose you work in a bakery. Are you merely making cakes? Or are you making delights that will enhance the celebration when folk get together?

Someone may say, "But I work in a mailroom. With little formal education, this is likely where I will work for the rest of my life. What possibility is there for me to invest my work with noble intention and to do something significant for others?"

If you work in a mailroom, you may wish to expand your service territory. Hold to the intent to be of greater use in some way that fulfills you. Plant the mustard seed of noble intent and see what happens. In the meantime, hold to the intent to continue in gainful employment in order to support your family—a noble activity. If you have no family to support, hold to the intent to continue to be self-supporting—again, a noble thing.

There is something else you can do. You can intend to be a radiating center of love in your workplace, bringing a smile and warm acceptance to all you encounter.

PRACTICE

Each morning set a noble intention for the day. At the end of the day, revisit your intention and give thanks that it guided and positively impacted your day.

GOALS VERSUS NOBLE INTENTION

There is a difference between setting a goal and setting an intention. Goals originate in the human mind, are quite defined, and are accomplished by mental willpower and physical effort. Therefore, they have limited possibilities. Intent is more general, equally focused but open to all positive possibilities.

With a goal, you imagine the desired outcome and work assiduously step-by-step to achieve it. With intent, you abandon any "efforting" to make specific things happen. You don't need to know how things are going to work out, you just need to trust that they will. Intention utilizes a more refined and powerful creative vibration than setting a goal and carrying it out. Intent requires that you set your intention, then hold to it, hold to it, hold to it—with all your heart.

How do you establish a noble intention? You cannot manufacture a noble intention, cannot just "think one up." You cannot pluck one out of the air, either. You don't look for a good cause and decide to get involved because it would be a good thing to do. Willing an intention into being is just another form of the thinking mind trying to be in control.

A noble intention has to come from the heart—*your* heart. Hence, noble intentions are highly personal. They are born at the core of your Being, the place where your everyday experience of your true Self interfaces with universal consciousness.

If you are coming from your heart, ask yourself, "How can I bring myself the greatest joy and fulfillment?" If you ask sincerely, you will receive an answer. This is guaranteed. How could it be otherwise, since you are asking your One Self, which would never deny you any good thing. Everything that could bring you peace, joy, and love is waiting for you to experience as you grow in higher consciousness. Universal consciousness knows what you need even before you are aware of it yourself. As such, many of us have experienced saying, "Thank you, my true Self, for having answered before I have even asked."

We can recognize a noble intention because it comes out of the purity of inner stillness and is not weighed down by thought forms. Noble intentions are made known to us when we listen to that still small voice within. The key is to be able to hear this inner voice of spirit. We can recognize this voice because it comes from a deeper place than the voices we usually hear in our head, and it carries the energy of our heart. This requires a certain amount of discernment.

To discern is quite different from trying to figure things out. It is a "knowing." The characteristic of this "knowing" is that it is devoid of ego. You will know you are receiving your answer when, instead of responding by imagining yourself successful, powerful, or wealthy, it has the confirming sense of a purpose that makes you a most loving, most joyful, most fulfilled self.

During the stage of creation through noble intent, all the action takes place on the inner dimension. The intention needs to be sustained by your heart energy. It is in sustaining it that you add the fuel that provides the power for its manifestation. Sometimes your intent is in the foreground, sometimes in the background, but it is always there until it produces the manifestation.

Setting a noble intention is not a one-time act. Ego can creep into even a noble intention if the intent is not sustained continually.

When you have a noble intention that runs throughout your life, it is likely part of your soul mission for this incarnation. In such a case, the noble intention remains constant, while the *form* of its expression will likely change over your lifetime. As you sustain your noble intention, life will predictably present you with more challenging and expansive ways to be of service. Your sphere of influence will likely also continue to increase, reaching larger and larger communities as the noble intention is sustained. Remember Jabez?

PRACTICE

When it emanates from your heart, set a noble intention. Write it down. Hold to the intention of it manifesting but not in a certain way. Note the timing of its manifestation. Note how you felt after this.

PRACTICE

Set a goal. Write it down. Work on achieving it. Note the timing of its completion. Note how you felt after achieving it.

THE POWER OF JOINING IN NOBLE INTENTION

Everywhere we look, life teaches us the powerful outcome of joining—atoms to molecules, seed with soil, sperm with egg, yeast with flour. It is in joining that our bodies and all forms of life beyond the single cell amoeba are created. This is so obvious that often we don't stop to marvel at the wonderment of creation.

Joining with another or others in noble intent is a sacred act. It is a partnership of souls who join without selfish motive, hidden agendas, or wobbly commitment. When two or more join in loving intent, out of the conjoined heart energy comes greater creativity. The creative power of love, present in each person who aligns with the same intent, supports and propels it into manifestation. When there is true joining of hearts, the power to quickly manifest a right outcome multiplies according to the numbers involved in the sacred joining and the strength of the spiritual energy charge each holds behind the common intent.

This is the kind of power that can quickly change our reality. When atoms join to form molecules, for example, a powerful laser-like energy is emitted. Similarly, when we join with others in noble intent, we let loose a powerful positive transformational force into our world.

Suppose you are an architect joining with city planners, a priest joining with a congregation, or a doctor joining with a patient. How can you know whether you are joining nobly? When egos join, they usually do so because they want something *from* the other, not *for* the other. Since noble intention does not come from ego, there is no selfishness in the parties who join together in it.

Since noble intention emanates from your true Self, when you join with another(s), you are joining them in Oneness. This is one of the quickest and most confirming ways to experience our

Oneness. Opportunities to experience Oneness in joint intention are everywhere. They are often found with what on the surface may seem like the most unlikely partners.

There are no boundaries and no impediments to joining in intent. Gender, age, nationality, religion, or geographical distance do not enter the picture. In intent, we can experience the reality of our Oneness with anyone, anywhere in the world. Through such joining, we tap into the Power of Oneness.

15

ACCESSING HIGHER CONSCIOUSNESS

INNER KNOWER – OUR SOURCE OF RELIABLE GUIDANCE

You have already read references to our Inner Knower in this book. Now, let us gain a deeper understanding of it.

Seeking advice from others for our consideration, listening to what we can learn from them, and reading books on what has caught our curiosity are normal and on balance positive actions. However, to rely solely on such things is to miss the most important and ever-present source of our inner wisdom and guidance.

We all have an Inner Knower who knows the Truth about all things – for us individually and for all of creation. It knows the way forward for all at all times. Our Inner Knower resides in the unified field of consciousness. Because it is not bound by time and space, it sees the whole picture, so to speak – the past, present, and what will present itself as the future. As we know, it is only when we go deep within ourselves, we discover another dimension—the realm of inner stillness. Awareness of our true Self emerges from this state. This is the home of our Inner Knower, which contains no limiting thoughts, beliefs, assumptions. It has full awareness of everything – of all that exists, has existed and exists in eternal potential. And it is from this source that helpful guidance and true insight arises.

Our Inner Knower isn't separate from us. On the contrary, it is a facet of our true Self. Some refer to it as their Higher Self, their True Being, their Awakened Self or the indwelling Holy Spirit. Our Inner Knower is more easily accessed when we are in a state of stillness. This is why it has often been referred to as "a still small voice," which we have been urged to listen for and listen to. Its voice is so different from that of the ego, which is loud, so loud at times, we can't hear anything but it.

Our consciousness isn't separate from the unified field of consciousness, rather we embody it. Consequently, there is nothing we face in our private lives or that we face in the world to which our Inner Knower does not have the perfect answer or response. The insight we experience from our Inner Knower comes as a "felt" knowing that can't necessarily be explained.

When we look at things through the eyes of ego, we tend to misperceive things. This is why our Inner Knower often speaks to us by correcting our perception. A correct perception may not bring about a change in our outer situation, but it will bring about a different way of seeing a situation that results in a sense of peace. So when we are not at peace, let's ask our Inner Knower to correct our perception about the situation or person so that we will experience peace. Once we have experienced the shift to correct perception, we often feel within ourselves that nothing in our outer world has changed, but everything has changed for us now that we see things differently. This shift can come about almost instantly and often seems miraculous.

The reason we experience peace when our Inner Knower corrects our perception is that peace is an aspect of our true nature. When we experience inner peace, we know we are seeing with accurate vision. Whenever we aren't at peace, our vision is skewed.

When we react to a situation or person with anger, resentment, criticism, or defensiveness, it's a cue to turn to our Inner Knower and ask what has not been healed within us yet that causes us to project our pain outward. When the answer comes – which it will in its own time – then let us ask to be shown the way to heal the root of the emotional wound we are still feeling.

When posing a major life issue question to our Inner Knower such as should we leave our partner, should we quit our job and go back to school, should we sell our home and move to another community, we likely will have to "sit" with our question for some time. It may be that we are not yet ready to hear the answer because it's not one our ego wants to hear and will reject. In such a situation, it's likely our guidance will come in stages. Why? Usually because our Inner Knower never reveals anything to us too early, never anything that may overwhelm us or cause us fear. It always knows what we are prepared to accept at a given time.

When we receive guidance from our Inner Knower, we find ourselves relaxing into a situation, a relationship, or life in general. We feel more expansive, more confident, clearer in our direction – and often we find the courage to act, which we never thought we had.

Just as we can't take a train ride without first buying a ticket, we can't receive answers from our Inner Knower unless we pose questions to It. Start by asking your Inner Knower where to find your glasses, your car keys, or what is important for you to see in a serial dream you have been having. Ask for help in writing a paper for your English Literature class, then watch the inspiration flow. The answer may come almost immediately or take some time. My experience has been the more often we turn to our Inner Knower for an answer, the quicker we receive it. And the higher our consciousness is, meaning the more we are attuned to our true Self, the more our Inner Knower can reveal to us.

Ask the question, then let it go – with ease and confidence. As stated, sometimes the answer comes immediately, at other times it takes a while. Listen and watch. Why watch? Because our Inner Knower often answers us through incidents that occur in our lives: repetitive occurrences, synchronicities, people we encounter, what others may say to us, and "signs" that may come to us from various sources – including nature.

How can we know when an answer is coming from our Inner Knower? When our Inner Knower responds to us, again, we will know it to be the authentic voice of our spirit because there will be a feeling of certainty about it and it is not accompanied by fear. Instead, we will relax into the "knowing". When it is right for us, there is no uncertainty, no further questioning, no room for doubt or hesitation. And after, there will be no doubt that we have made the right decision, have taken the right action. Having said this, the ego may still try to interfere through evoking doubt or fear, but we now know how to detect the ego and can choose to listen to the "right" voice, that of your loving, omniscient Inner Knower. If we are guided by our Inner Knower to take action, it will be action likely done with grace and ease. It will lead to healing or some other positive outcome, not only for ourselves but for all concerned.

The more often we ask for guidance from our Inner Knower and to correct a perception, the more readily we develop our "inner ears" to hear its voice and the more confident we become in living our life from the inside out—as it was always meant to be lived. This security is needed especially in these times of confusion and high uncertainty. With the widespread availability of information through various forms of media and the worldwide web, never before have there been so many outside voices to listen to, and never before have they seemed to be more varied and conflicting. We need the discernment our Inner Knower can give us.

WHEN YOU DON'T KNOW HOW TO PRAY FOR SOMEONE

Often we are concerned about our loved ones but don't really know what is best for them. Consequently, we are at a loss for how to pray for them. For example, if a person is very aged, should we pray that they be physically healed or that they find the grace to leave their body peacefully? At such times, it is a relief to know we don't have to be clear on what is best for the person we care about. We can turn our concern over to our Inner Knower.

In such a situation, our prayer may go something like this. "Inner Knower, I don't know how to pray for _____, so I ask you to in silence and in stillness to pray the perfect prayer for them. Then simply rest in the stillness, knowing that your Inner Knower realizes what is the highest and best for your loved one and all concerned.

WHAT PREVENTS US FROM CONNECTING WITH OUR INNER KNOWER?

One of the blocks we experience to receiving guidance from our Inner Knower is our tendency to seek answers mainly outside ourselves. In our world, idolatry of individuals who are considered leading lights in society is rampant, as attested to by our glorification of politicians, celebrities, movie stars, wealthy executives, sports and entertainment figures.

Anyone who is lionized by the masses knows they have no absolute answers to give others. Yet very few of them tell their supporters or fans to turn their attention away from them and back to themselves. However, this is what the true spiritual teacher always says. "Don't look at me; don't adulate me," says the true teacher. "See the magnificence in your own essence. Know that you already know what I can share with you."

When another tells you something about yourself, this is not the same as self-discovery. Unless your own consciousness grasps the truth of the observation or insight expressed by another, it doesn't have the power to transform you. Others may point the way or mirror something to you about yourself, but only to the degree that what someone shares triggers your own inner knowing does it liberate you from your conditioning. We have become so influenced by the external world that we rarely look inside ourselves for direction. Yet here alone do we meet the causative dimension of our experiences. Guidance must come from within. Most of us have heard the expression, "When the student is ready, the teacher will appear." The readiness of the student is everything. Readiness is partly based on our connection with our Inner Knower; then, we are more likely to recognize and benefit from a true spiritual or other kind of valuable teacher.

Neither is guidance assured by following certain practices. Just as we fall into different metabolic types, so we also have different temperaments and therefore find some practices helpful and others unproductive. Because we are all unique, a practice that is helpful to one may be a form of irritation to another. Only when a technique feels comfortable, feels easy for us, is it helpful in facilitating the awareness and expression of our authentic Being.

You might imagine that your beliefs are a safe guide. However, think about how a person's beliefs may evolve during the course of a lifetime. For example, many of us find ourselves holding quite different beliefs in mid-life from those we held when we were young. In addition, one of the impediments to personal growth is holding on to the ideologies we were programmed with. Some evident examples are: the person who always votes conservatively because three generations of their family have; rigid belief in the religion we practice without accepting or honoring the religious practices of others; feeling we must be doing something wrong or not deserving if we don't experience financial abundance in our life or meet the "right" partner.

Many of us are not yet in the habit of seeking guidance from our Inner Knower, preferring to stay with the more familiar approaches of asking advice from family and friends, reading books, or relying on what we think of as our "feelings", which are too often conditioned emotions emanating from conditioned thoughts, rather than caring guidance emanating from the wisdom of our Inner Knower. Having said this, our Inner Knower may guide us to seek professional help to identify and facilitate the healing of our "wounds".

Our Inner Knower uses and speaks to us through our strong heart based bonds. I once was sitting in my living room and without thinking suddenly jumped up and ran to the corner only to see my daughter who was in grade two at the time, trying to cross one of the busiest streets in Vancouver without being at the cross lights. I yelled to her to go back to the corner and cross the street safely.

Many examples of such occurrences have been written about. Take the examples of a mother knowing the instant her son died in a war a continent away; or the dog whose owner had gone on a supposedly 3-week work trip thousands of miles away that was cut short so he could return after 10 days. As soon as that was determined, his dog went to the door and started waiting for his beloved owner.

Opposites don't attract. Like attracts like. For example, often unconscious people are not attracted to conscious people and vice-versa. I once asked a woman what she loved most about her husband. She responded, "His strength, his integrity, and his goodness." What she couldn't see at that time was that she too embodied these qualities. We cannot see in another what we do not already embody in ourselves. It took a number of years for her to come to this realization. As she did, I noticed that her husband was also realizing that he embodied the things he most loved about his wife. When we genuinely fall in love with someone, we are seeing through the outer to their inner beauty, to the essence of the person, which draws us because it is a reflection of our own inner beauty and laudable traits.

This principle of recognizing our self in others applies even when an angry, negative person is attracted to a spiritually peaceful person.

Beneath their negativity, there is an unconscious awareness of their own fundamentally peaceful and loving Self. If this weren't the case, they would not be attracted to the peace and love expressed by another.

If you see a number of angry people in your life, how can you know whether you are projecting your anger onto them and they are just mirroring it back to you, or they are being attracted to your inner peace and want to drop their anger and experience it too? Ask your Inner Knower.

OUR INNER GROWER

Our Inner Grower is an aspect of our Inner Knower. It is really Consciousness Itself looking for greater expression through our human form. If we listen to our Inner Knower, our Inner Grower won't need to be as active.

HOW DO WE KNOW WHEN OUR INNER GROWER IS AT WORK?

Often we know our Inner Grower is at work because we feel an inner dissonance, an inexplicable dis-ease or what some have referred to as "divine discontent" – divine because it calls us forth to grow in consciousness and character. It is felt like an inner creative tension: a pull-like invitation from where we currently are to where we need to go to grow, although most often, at first, this is at an unconscious level. It often takes time for our Inner Grower to bring this into our awareness.

Take the incident of the woman who suddenly didn't feel

completely satisfied in her career anymore. She felt some inner disturbing feelings but could not identify why. She asked her Inner Knower and one day soon after she woke up said to herself, "I want to have a baby!"

Sometimes surprise is what is experienced when your Inner Grower is active: surprise that you do want to have children after all; surprise that you want to write a book; surprise that you want to take up painting when you can't even draw; surprise that you want to join a spiritual community; surprise that after 10 years of priesthood you want to leave and enter civil community.

Our Inner Grower works to get us unstuck from various aspects of our "woundedness" or when our ego needs to be tamed, so as to prompt us to further personal growth and spiritual realization. Sometimes we get ourselves into challenging situations — and I use the expression "get ourselves into" deliberately — because at some level we know we need these situations for our ongoing spiritual development. On the one hand, it sounds mad to us that we would do such, but in reality, it comes from our Inner Grower's wisdom and Self-love.

When our Inner Grower is at work, we can experience some anxiety but accompanying this is also the need to grow into a more conscious person. And the latter, if we follow the prompting of our Inner Grower, will bring us to a new state of growth and happiness.

Our Inner Grower only intimates or suggests movement. It does not push us. We are always given a choice — the comfortable pew versus the pull of the unknown. Ambivalence is often a common feeling when our Inner Grower is at work tilling our inner soil.

Additionally, some degree of discontent is also involved. Do we allow it just to be or do we repress it, thereby letting it prevent our experiencing a new awareness or growth of some nature? This is a germane question. The more one gives into a reluctance of growing to be a more conscious human being, the more likely one's discontent will persist. Most people who have moved with the prompting of their Inner Grower say that for them, *not* to address the cause of their inner dissonance is actually more painful and ironically fearful than not taking a risk. For them, stagnation is their greatest fear.

Usually we are called to take small, incremental but challenging growth steps. If we don't pay attention to these directions from our Inner Grower to take these smaller steps, over time, these accumulate. Then our Inner Grower may be prepared to give us a huge wake-up call, to take us into all nature of pain if that is what is necessary to shock us out or our egoic self-centered mindset and into our heart.

THE PARABLE OF TWO BABY EAGLES

I remember reading about a parable that can serve to illustrate how our Inner Grower can work to shock us into action.

A devoted servant wanted to express his gratitude to his master by giving him his two prized possessions – baby eagles. The master was delighted with the gift and instructed his servant to put the two baby eagles on the tree outside his house so he could see them every day.

Within a few days, one of the baby eagles took flight, bringing much delight to the master as he watched it soar with ease then return to the branch. The other baby eagle did not fly. A full week passed, but it still sat perched in the same place on the same branch.

Seeing this, the servant became upset and visited his Master to apologize for giving him an eagle that would not fly. "I will replace it as soon as I can, vowed the servant."

"Nonsense," said the Master. "There is nothing wrong with that eagle." Having nothing but the best interests of the bird at heart and knowing its capability, the master took a saw from his toolshed and cut off the branch to which that baby eagle clung. Up and away it flew – even higher than the other eagle.

Most of us at some time in our lives are like the second baby eagle that clung to his comfortable branch out of fear of taking a risk to fly, to fully live. If we were lucky, we were in touch with our Inner Grower who, without our awareness, cut the branch or provided a life event or placed someone in our life to do it for us.

I know a woman who left her home town after high school, went to university, got married, was active in doing different things, and continued to grow spiritually throughout her life. She had the experience one summer of returning to her hometown and visited a familiar park she played in throughout her youth. She related that in that park – which really had not changed in any significant way during the many years she was away – she experienced the same familiar scenes and feelings she did 30 years earlier. Then a thought crossed her mind: "What if I had never moved?" I could have been limited to experiencing just this one park when throughout my life, so far I have already experienced hundreds.

People who respond to their Inner Grower often recount incidents like this.

PRACTICE

Do you recall a time when you didn't listen to the prompting of your Inner Grower? If so, what was the result? Conversely, do you recall a time when you did listen to your Inner Grower. If so, what was the result?

16

MAJOR IMPEDIMENTS TO INNER PEACE

THE PAIN-BODY

A wonderful man in a happy marriage is strongly concerned because he loves his children deeply yet can't stop himself from often yelling at them in anger then feeling terrible after doing so. The last thing he wants to do is hurt or upset his children. But no matter how he tries to treat his children in a more loving way, his angry behavior persists. This is his pain-body in unconscious action.

One of Eckhart Tolle's major contributions as a spiritual teacher was to bring our attention to what he calls the "pain-body". Spiritual teacher Barry Long also talked about the pain-body.

I have come to see there is more to understand about the pain-body. Yes, it is repressed pain and knows only pain, so energetically is able to stay alive and grow only by creating more pain. This causes many upsets and problems. However, I believe, it wants to be released but doesn't know how to do so without creating more pain for others and accumulating more pain for itself. Just as when you ingest some contaminated food, your body throws it off through vomiting or throws off a bacteria by creating a high temperature to kill it, the pain-body too, I believe, wants to be relieved of its pain. But most of us don't know how to help it dissipate or relinquish its painful emotional energy.

The pain-body consists of repressed but alive emotional pain held within the physical body. Although not a solid entity, it is very real and a very powerful energetic field in its ability to quickly bring up unconscious pain from our past and in ways that can take us over, meaning take us into a state of not being in control.

We all have a pain-body made up of repressed emotional pain from our past that seeks whatever way it can to be released. When in the womb and especially in early childhood when we were non-conceptual and non-verbal therefore unable to understand why we felt awful at times nor able to give expression to our agitated state, we couldn't do anything. We couldn't flee or fight, only freeze the negative emotional energy charges in our body because we were helpless in the world of adults, especially with our parents and other authority figures.

This unconscious repressed emotional pain accumulated over time. As it built up and gained in energy, it waited for any catalyst or "trigger" to bring some of it to the surface to be released. But before we knew this is what was happening to us, when the emotional pain held within us was triggered by a person, incident, even such a thing as a smell, we took the surfacing pain that was triggered and projected it onto someone or some situation. It came out as expressed anger, blame, or an upset of some kind. In such situations, our pain-body sadly doesn't dissipate some of its held pain but creates more pain – for itself and others.

We know it is the pain-body at work when a minor incident can provoke an exaggerated and often volatile response, usually in the form of anger or attack. Or it can surface as a sudden feeling of sadness or depression which has no apparent external cause.

Whenever you feel you can't help yourself and just lost it, it is likely the pain-body that is active and has taken you over, so to speak. You really aren't in control of these unconscious emotions that are arising – unless you are aware of the pain-body and are able to witness it when it arises.

Take the incident of a person going into an anger fit because their partner forgot their birthday. It could be this person was significantly ignored by one or both parents when younger and the missed recognition of their birthday triggered the repressed pain of feeling insignificant, even to the point of often feeling invisible around their parents. The person who forgot the birthday, however, will bear the brunt of this person's pain-body.

Take another incident such as a man going to work every day and dreading having to walk by the windowed office of his boss in order to get to his desk. Every time he walks by, he feels angry at his boss. Of course, this interferes with his relationship with him. One day, however, he stopped to ask himself why this negative reaction to his boss persisted and with no apparent reason, since his boss only acted reasonably with him. If he knew about the pain-body, he would likely immediately know that it was not his boss he disliked, but because his boss's facial features reminded him of his father who verbally abused him and put him down when he was a child, he was actually projecting onto his boss his repressed anger at his father. Once he realizes this, his discomfort of walking by his boss's office will stop and his relationship with him become more positive.

Because the pain-body can wreak such havoc in people's lives and wants to be released, is there a HOW to help it dissipate?

Yes, first by accepting that you and everyone has a pain-body. Once you have recognized the pain-body in yourself, you have already broken identification with it as who you are, thereby weakening its power to throw you off balance. Then you can also recognize the pain-body in others when it is active and understand it is not really who they are. Understanding and forgiveness of self and others is greatly enhanced when we understand this.

Be vigilant and notice when your pain-body is activated and ask yourself, "When last did I feel this emotional pain and overreact?" Then ask, "When was the first time I felt this kind of pain?" You may not be able to remember the first time you felt this pain and likely not able to identify the source of it. However, just by asking these questions, you are giving your subconscious the opportunity to answer for you. You may be aware of the answer when it comes or not. You don't have to be. You will know there is a measure of release at the root of this pain when you no longer react to that particular situation or trigger as you have in the past.

Be the still observer of the negative emotion from the pain-body arising in you before it turns into a thought that justifies its expression. Identify it as such and try not to give it free rein to act out. In this way, you attempt to catch the pain-body before it does damage. At first you may not be successful in doing this and only able to witness the aftermath of the damage it caused you and others. Then next, you may be able to witness the pain-body as it starts to act through you and stop it at the beginning or in the middle of its expression. In this way, you are starting to dissipate it.

By simply breaking personal identification with the pain-body and observing it when it arises, you are not further repressing but helping to release it. Next, when you feel the pain-body starting to become active, stay in the present moment and go into stillness. The pain-body is from the held past in you. The past and present cannot exist at the same time in your consciousness. And in stillness no emotional or psychic pain can touch you. Most importantly, embrace the formerly unconscious pain in you in a state of Presence. However, do not go into thinking. Stay with the sensation, however uncomfortable it feels, then bring the energy of consciousness within the inner body to the pain you feel and hold it in the arms of your Presence. Keep your full-body felt attention in the Now. Hold the uncomfortable energy. Hold it. Hold it as if you are holding an innocent infant in your hands and refusing to drop it. Hold the pain until it is released by the power of your Presence. This is a powerful practice that for some may take time to master. Keep with it. Each time you hold the uncomfortable energy of the pain-body in you that arises with your Presence, if only for a short time at first, you are helping to diminish it, neutralize it, or transform it into peace.

THE COLLECTIVE PAIN-BODY

There is also a collective pain-body made up of the accumulated repressed emotional pain over time of communities such as families, cities, countries, and also our Mother Earth itself. The collective pain-body can range from being rather light to being very heavy. Just ask someone what they felt when they entered another's home or got off an airplane in a certain country, and they will be able to express either a lightness of being, a feeling of neutrality, or a heaviness weighing them down.

In terms of the collective pain-body, because of our Oneness, we all are affected by all. This cannot be repeated often enough. When one human suffers, we all to some degree suffer. When there is a mass shooting in London, a terrorist attack in France, a famine in Africa, destructive floods, earthquakes, tsunamis, forest-fires, and life-taking epidemics—wherever they occur on the planet—we all feel to some degree the pain experienced by those in our human family who have suffered the effects. Depending on how open and sensitive we are, we may sometimes feel this pain acutely.

However, most of us aren't aware that the reason we feel sad or anxious or depressed for seemingly no personal reason can be related to our picking up our individual portion of the collective pain-body. It is a wise practice to try to discern if the emotional pain we are experiencing at any one time is coming from our personal or collective pain-body.

HOW do we deal with the collective pain-body? By recognizing it as such and sending our love and compassion and prayers to our suffering fellow humans. In addition, we can accept, without resistance, that suffering is still part of our human experience at this time. Keep in mind that in our Oneness because we are affected by the pain of our brothers and sisters, we are also able in our Oneness to effect healing for them as well.

FEELING IT TO HEAL IT

Besides holding repressed emotional pain from our past, we also hold pain from unresolved or not fully expressed fear, anger and grief.

A woman explained she got so angry at another driver who almost hit her that the ferocity of her anger shocked her. A caring professional in the alternative health industry, she asked, "Do I really hold such fierce anger within me?" The answer, of course is "Yes", because if she didn't hold it within in her, she couldn't have expressed it.

So many of us are like this woman who never felt safe enough to express honest anger even in a way that could hurt no one. As children we were not allowed to get angry with our parents, teachers, elders, figures of authority. If we did, there would be consequences to pay. We are often given "permission" to express many of our emotions to others or in public, but not anger. The woman mentioned who was almost hit by a car was deeply fearful for her life and her fear came out as anger, which is what surprised her.

Everyone goes through the grieving process in their own unique way, and it will take as long as it takes. A woman I know who lost her beloved husband seemed to grieve in a quiet and balanced fashion. When I pointed this out to her, she responded by telling me that this was not so, that she often had to go into her car, lock the doors and scream out her anger or grief so that no one could hear her. She felt she had to release her pain, and a safe way to do it without hurting others or bringing them down was to verbalize, scream and cry out her grief in private.

In our fast-paced, highly demanding world, many of us don't take time to fully go through the grieving process when we lose someone close to us. Yes, we acknowledge our grief, then often quickly put it to the side as best we can and get on with the demands of our life. We often consciously repress grief because it feels too painful and interferes with our "pressing on" in life. However, grief not expressed will live on in the energy body and eventually bring about an imbalance in aspects of our physical, emotional, or mental states.

TRAUMA

Trauma of any kind, be it a car accident, a surprising deep betrayal, war experience, witnessing a heinous act, being bullied, having a concussion, prenatal and early childhood trauma, and so forth, so shocks our body and very being that we cannot take the trauma in at the time it occurs. This creates an imbalance and vulnerability within us.

Trauma affects our mental, emotional, and physical bodies, down to every one of our cells. Our being wants to free itself of such imbalance. When animals in the wild experience trauma, once the danger has passed, they literally shake off the energy of fear - of fight or flight. We have witnessed ample examples of this personally or on television. But HOW can we shake it off? If we aren't able to shake it off physically at the time we experience the trauma, the body later tries to shake it off for us. We literally start shaking for what we feel is for no reason: our hands shake, our eyes twitch, our legs tremble, we feel dizzy. This surfacing energy is also usually felt in the body as an uncomfortable energy force, a vibration of sorts.

Many feel it in the stomach and solar plexus areas, but it can awaken in other parts of our body as well.

If we are not aware of what is happening to us, we will be puzzled, upset, alarmed. The recently coined medical term for this is "body anxiety". Peter Levine did pioneering research in the area of somatic healing, which means healing the nervous system after the experience of trauma. He provides many helpful practices to release trauma from the body. His two seminal books in this area are referenced in the Recommended Reading section at the back of this book.

17

FORGIVENESS BRINGS PEACE

Forgiveness involves compassion and brings us the gift of peace. Non-forgiveness is a form of revenge or payback that only causes hurt to the other and ourselves. Don't try to pay back in kind. To step up to hurt and respond with understanding and kindness will bring about blessings to all concerned, although the deemed perpetrator may not realize it at the time.

What wisdom we hold in hindsight! To grow up, we were prone to make lots of "mistakes". But as adults, we have the advantage of looking in the rear-view mirror, so to speak. More often than not, we realize that these "mistakes" were essential to our development. Set against a backdrop of our evolution as human beings, the things we call mistakes also take on new meanings. They often become hidden gifts to be unwrapped and examined. Times when we miss the mark and end up experiencing guilt and regret are opportunities to be thankful for, as they alert us to areas of our lives in which we still need healing or to express the loving person we truly are.

Ask your Inner Knower to show you where in your life you are withholding love from yourself and others. Then, watch what emerges not only from within, as your awareness expands, but also in the circumstances of your outer experiences. You will see that the situations you find yourself in mirror back to you the precise areas of your life where your love has flourished and other areas where it still needs to do so.

A common misperception is that if one forgives another, they are somehow better than the other for doing so. Yes, the other person is still "guilty", but we found it in ourselves to forgive them anyway. This is another form of the ego fostering separation by feeling superior. We all need forgiveness at times. We all mess up, because on the human level we are not flawless.

We realize that the many times we "get it wrong" are how we learn to act with authenticity, responsibility, and integrity next time. From an evolutionary standpoint, there never was a time in which individuals and the world were flawless. On the contrary, evolution proceeds by making the flawed into the less flawed. At the personal and social levels, when we hurt badly enough from our choices, we eventually no longer wish to be hurt or hurtful and begin making better choices.

When asked how often we should forgive, the Master Jesus responded, "Seventy times seven", meaning without end.[1] He understood that we and others come into our own through trial and error and that sometimes we all will make poor choices and often countless times before we discover the advantages of becoming more responsible.

No matter how many times we create painful situations for ourselves and others, there are no scales to balance. There is only Self, which includes a person or situation to which we need to extend our love in a fuller way than we have been capable of until now.

Still, there is an aspect of forgiveness that encourages us to turn to our brother or sister and express our desire for their forgiveness. This is lovely. We are saying, "I would like another opportunity to show you what a loving person I truly am, because I have not shown you this about myself." So we pick up the telephone or we buy the bouquet of flowers that has "sorry" written all over it— and if possible, we make reparations. This is not "undoing" some supposed wrongdoing but simply moving forward in expressing the love that is our true nature.

Having said this, you can forgive but not necessarily re-establish a relationship. A woman chose to part from her two aunts earlier in her life because they came from such judgment and negativity. Years later she received a surprising card in the mail asking for forgiveness from one of them. In truth, she could not remember the specifics of what the aunts had said and done to cause her to move away from their energy. She replied with a card, stating that she could remember nothing that needed to be forgiven, but was happy to extend her forgiveness if the aunts felt they needed to hear it.

It was clear that the aunts wanted to restore their relationship with her. However, the niece knew it was not appropriate for her to go back into that relationship. Her Inner Knower told her that to extend an invite to meet with her aunts now would not have been authentic and therefore not in spiritual integrity. Forgiveness is given and received on a higher level than human drama. Whether two people consider restoring a relationship is then a matter of choice, guided by your Inner Knower.

Whether a relationship is restored or not, what a gift mutual forgiveness brings to our brothers and sisters, as each of us is blessed with a sense of promoting each other's well-being along this evolutionary journey.

WHY FORGIVING OURSELVES IS DIFFICULT

The majority of us find it easier to forgive others than to forgive ourselves. This is because others' judgment of us can still cause us self-doubt or is deeply embedded in our subconscious from infancy, a young age, and perhaps even from past lifetimes. What is the source of such self-judgment? Often it is because we have internalized the voices of these "outside" critics. Because of this, we also find it hard to love ourselves unconditionally.

Michael Brown points out in his book *The Presence Process* that we are unconditional love born into a conditional world that withholds unconditional love from us. This causes us to believe we are broken, not good enough, unworthy, even bad. If we didn't believe this, we would naturally experience self-love.

Seeking unconditional love from others is like looking for a breath of fresh air in the depths of the ocean, says Michael Brown. He adds that, "If we want to experience a breath of fresh air in the depths of the ocean, we had better make sure we place it there ourselves."[2] How do we find unconditional love in a conditional world? Michael Brown tells us we have to give it to ourselves and keep giving it and giving it until self-love prevails. This is not being narcissistic. It is a precondition for unconditional love for others because such begins with unconditional love for oneself.

We also find it hard to forgive ourselves because to do so means we will have to drop the kind of egoic thinking that tells us we should be better, when it actually makes us vulnerable to the negative energy of self-judgment. Our conditioned mind says, "You need to be a good person. You need to be perfect in order to be lovable and loved. If you are good, you will be safe." Of course, as soon as we are not perfect, we feel unsafe. Fear takes over. We may be afraid of punishment or simply afraid for no particular reason. As long as the egoic mind holds us in the grip of fear, we cannot love ourselves unconditionally.

One of our greatest fears is of receiving a whipping from our egoic self. Self-criticism perpetuates the strength of the punishing ego because it keeps us in a state of weakness and fear. When we repeat a negative behavior and continue to beat ourselves up after each "lapse", the worse we feel about ourselves and the more likely we are to repeat the negative behavior to reinforce our low self-concept. Beating ourselves up only fosters the negative behavior to continue. It's the proverbial vicious circle.

Most self judgment is irrational. Just listen to your self-talk around self judgment and see how absolutely unproductive it is. Why do we do this? It's from our irrational self judgment and accompanying lack of self forgiveness that we create much of our inner drama. Negative self-talk feeds drama. When our negative self-talk stops, we feel calmer and our drama falls away, making room for inner peace. Of course, the ego will fight to prevent this, since drama is a decoy that prevents us from coming from our authentic self. This is another reason why it is usually easier to forgive others than to forgive ourselves. When we look at others, we don't hear the self-judgmental mental chatter going on in our head.

But most importantly, when we judge and criticize ourselves, we don't know yet who we truly are: extensions of our true Source and already and always perfect.

BUT YOU HURT ME

We are able to forgive others when we recognize that at the time they caused us hurt through insensitivity, cruelty, abandonment, betrayal it was because they were not yet ready to come from a level of caring consciousness. This then makes it easier to forgive ourselves as well, because when we hurt another, we too realize we were not coming from such a level of caring consciousness. Hence, we all did the best we could coming from our level of consciousness at the time. When we become ready to forgive others and ourselves, this is evidence that we have grown in consciousness. Celebrate this.

The following illustrates why we need to forgive and be forgiven. It also fosters a sense of being alike and therefore moves us closer to realizing our Oneness.

"I TOO"

In unconsciousness:

You have lied to me. I too have lied to others.

You have let me down. I too have let down others.
You have disappointed me. I too have disappointed others.
You have hurt me. I too have hurt others.
You betrayed my trust. I too have betrayed others' trust.
You have disregarded my feelings. I too have disregarded others'
feelings
I forgive you. Would you please forgive me if I have done any of
the above to you.

PRACTICE

Now, think of someone you still find hard to forgive and write your
own "I Too" prayer based on your relationship with them.

You have _____. I too have _____.

Continue on until you feel completion in your entries.

Then at the end add, "I forgive you; would you please forgive me? If
you cannot forgive me, I forgive myself regardless."

PRACTICE

We need to start by forgiving others because as stated above, it is
easier to forgive others than ourselves.

Let our prayer be:

"I forgive anyone who has hurt me out of their unconsciousness at
the time." Then take a deep breath in and when you breathe out,
say to yourself, "I now release the negative energy surrounding this."

Then do the same regarding forgiving yourself for any hurt you have caused others through your unconsciousness at the time.

Just as we have been told we need to forgive "seventy times seven", we may need to say this prayer of forgiveness of others and ourselves many times until we drop the burdens of blame and guilt and feel the peace that will follow.

LOOKING AT FORGIVENESS FROM A HIGHER LEVEL

Our true Self holds no judgment. Forgiveness should flow easily because in the final analysis there is nothing to forgive. There is just the One Self taking on human form in a multitude of expressions and choosing to live through the messy process of coming into an understanding of who we truly are. As humans, we all mess up.

We forgive by seeing through the veil of illusion of separation from our Source and recognizing that in our true Self we are all flawless expressions of our Source. Since we are all One, there is no "other" to blame.

18

FURTHER IMPEDIMENTS TO INNER PEACE

"Yesterday I was clever, so wanted to change the world.
Today I am wise, so I am changing myself."

Rumi

VICTIMS ARE NOT PEACEFUL

When we think of ourselves as victims, we never heal. Because we see things as coming to us from outside of ourselves, we perceive ourselves as having little control over what happens to us. This generates fear, causes us to experience feelings of helplessness and incites us to blame someone or something else for our experiences.

By giving our power away to others and external circumstances, we cut ourselves off from the only true means of healing, and the only way to change our experiences, which are found within ourselves. And so we remain victims.

The root of feeling like a victim lies not in what happens to us from outside ourselves, but that we do not truly know ourselves and therefore love ourselves under all circumstances. I spent time with a Reiki Master. To him enlightenment meant we treat ourselves kindly and still love ourselves in our darkest moments. How profound. Self-love is not only a great healer but an indication of our knowing who we truly are.

To shed your victim mentality involves being with yourself and allowing yourself to feel your own love—no matter what may have happened or is happening to you. It involves feeling the love you are, in all the dimensions of your Being, especially those you have tended to disown.

When we start to embrace our true Self and allow ourselves to feel the unconditional love that is our very essence, we discover that we are not and never have been separate from our Source.

Yes, I hear you. You have been wronged, hurt unjustly. But your true Self cannot be hurt. You now have the opportunity to stand up for justice and perhaps even step up to helping others who have experienced the same kind of hurt you have endured. Ending a sense of victimhood involves no longer contracting into oneself but adopting an active energy to move forward, to do what you can to heal.

The good news is that you can always choose again. If you do not like some of what you have experienced or continue to experience, you can change it or at least your perception of it. This is how we heal ourselves and our world, since the world of form and what we experience are an "out-picturing" of our inner self-created reality.

PRACTICE
Before you get up in the morning, enter the inner body by

intentionally igniting the energy of consciousness within it all at once. This may take up to a minute. Then just be with who you truly are. Drop your roles, your story, your body-concept, and so forth. Release everything. Feel into your essence. Intentionally put your focus on your heart center and feel the warmth of the love inside you. Now, breathe the love that you are in and out from your heart center. No thinking is involved in this, only an intention to feel the love that you are.

JUDGMENT DOES NOT BRING US PEACE

When we judge, it is the ego leading the way to our feeling more than or less than others.

As stated, there is no room for judgment in higher consciousness. Fundamentally, all judgment stems from the erroneous belief that we are completely separate beings, needing to protect ourselves against other people, difficult situations, and painful experiences because we see ourselves as vulnerable to attack from outside forces – whether real or imaginary. In essence, we have judged that to be alive at all is to be at risk of attack from "out there". In concluding this, what we have really done is judge Life itself to be threatening and therefore something to be feared. And that is the kind of world we have created. When we do not believe in the benign, loving, supportive nature of Life, we severely limit our ability to experience Life as such.

Judging has become so interwoven into the fabric of our lives that we often are not aware we are doing it. There seems to be nothing that escapes our judgment—people, self, situations, and experiences.

Next time you walk down the street, notice how many times you judge the people you encounter only through your outer senses. "Gad, she's fat. He needs a haircut. That poor lonely man. Nice suit; he must be rich." When we judge, we are saying we don't want something in our life because we *think* it doesn't match our desires or expectations. Since the ego is perpetually not happy with things as they are, always wanting and needing more or something else, we take some of its "food" away when we stop judging.

Judging means we are resisting or envying, which closes the door to our receiving blessings or benefits from what or who we judge. Not judging opens the door to appreciation. If we have only a crust of bread to eat, we can judge it as not being sufficient or we can eat it with appreciation and gratitude thereby transforming it into a feast. If we begrudge the fact that we have only three dollars in our pocket, why would our true Self give us ten? Acceptance, appreciation, and gratitude open the floodgates for the abundance of our true Self to flow into our life.

We are never happy when we judge another because judgment separates us from our sisters and brothers, making us superior and the other inferior or vice versa. When we judge others, we are actually saying that we are right and they are wrong. This is an activity of ego, not of our loving Self. It fosters separation through disassociation or rejection. We can never be fully at peace when we have put another out of our heart. When we identify with our false egoic self, we believe that by attacking others via judgment we are able to make ourselves stronger and less vulnerable to attack from them. This is an illusion.

Judgment isolates and distorts because it never sees the whole and thereby what is good about the person or situation being judged. This includes when we judge ourselves. When receiving a single negative judgment from another, how often have we experienced that this one expressed negative takes over our whole self-concept for a period of time – even if we know it is not justified. That is all we can see at the time, forgetting we are not what people judge about us. The judging ego of others can take us to a state of forgetting the magnificence of our true Self. When we fall into this trap, we allow the criticizing ego of another to affect our vulnerable sense of self based on their ego.

If we judge a situation because it disturbs us, we realize again that we are in the hands of the ego. Of course, there is fact. And there is healthy caution, such as when we feel a place is not safe or in the presence of a highly negative or energy-draining person who is someone to be avoided.

"But what if I am suffering from a sore leg? Am I to bless this situation and be thankful for it?"

In any painful or upsetting situation, the most self-loving response is acceptance of it because this keeps us from falling into egoic fear. Again, as stated in an earlier chapter, acceptance is not resignation or inaction, but an opportunity to live more peacefully as we move with the flow of life – whatever life has to bring us at the time.

"What about when tragedy strikes?"

Ah, this is the acid test of whether we really have come into awareness of our true nature. If we can see through tragedy to the underlying larger plan of the One Self—if we truly believe that everything is love—then love, and only love, is what we will experience. We will find the succor, the good in tragedy. This is the treasure that is buried underneath pain. This is why it is usually at our lowest point, when in our deepest agony that we are visited by grace: that gentle, buoying energy that envelops, supports, and protects us while also giving us strength and reminding us that all is still well. Challenged by the human condition of being vulnerable in our bodies, the reality of our true Self breaks through to remind us that our body is not all we are but only a vehicle for experiencing our true Self in human form.

BLAME BE GONE

When we blame, we resist someone or something in our life because we feel they are responsible for our irritation, pain, or unhappiness.

When you don't blame the weather for the fact that you are feeling low, feeling sad, you may come to see that you are really "using" the grey, rainy day to help you release unexpressed pain over some loss in your life—perhaps the recent loss of your job or a beloved pet. In this way, you can acknowledge and be thankful for the healing process the dull day facilitates.

When you don't blame your parents for your feeling separation anxiety, you may come to see the root of it is your sense of separation from your true Self.

When you don't blame the dog for disturbing your sleep, you acknowledge your lack of sleep but don't mix it with anger and fuel it with resentment the following day, thereby increasing the drain on your energy.

Blaming puts up a wall that prevents us from seeing what we are creating in our lives and why. It is disempowering when we ascribe the control over our circumstances and feelings to someone or something else. When we feel justified in our blaming, we are just finding an excuse for not taking responsibility for our lives the way they are. It isn't possible to blame and feel empowered at the same time.

Take the incident of a daughter sitting with her aged father who had physically and emotionally abused her as a child. Although now as an adult she no longer feared him, she still couldn't see that anything good could come out of her relationship with him. On this occasion, her father was relating a story of receiving an anonymous letter from a person who criticized him for his behavior to his family. The father showed the letter to her, and feeling she did not want to add to his painful feelings of being judged, she just sat and listened to his words. She realized she may never again have time to sit with him alone before he died, and this time simply listened from inner stillness without resistance to him or judgment of any kind. She told me that soon she wasn't a daughter listening to her father or even a female listening to a male, but a field of Presence blending with another field of Presence. In that moment, she felt nothing but love for and Oneness with her father. This is spiritual communion. In this communion of Oneness, she found peace. When her father died, she was left with no regrets or lingering emotional pain from the past, just the reality of the love they both felt for each other in their experience of their Oneness.

This rare kind of incident surely can qualify as a reconciliation miracle and evidence of the power of grace in our lives. It also brings to mind the statement from *A Course In Miracles*: "The holiest of all the spots on earth is where an ancient hatred has become a present love."[1]

We can see that when we blame others for wrongdoings, faults, mistakes, we are often using them as scapegoats. Scapegoating is putting onto another the things we don't want to accept about ourselves and therefore an indirect means of self-attack, self-criticism, and even self-loathing. It is usually executed at an unconscious level. We blame another for the unconscious self-criticism we hold and project this onto them. When we blame with vehemence—when we don't own in any measure the fault we see in others—this is a signal that we are likely using another as a scapegoat. Our own negative state is being reflected back to us in how we see the other.

By using another as a scapegoat, we attempt to free ourselves of blame and responsibility. We are never free of the effects of our own actions—it is only an illusion to think that we are. As long as we are projecting our own internal issues onto others, we cannot be at peace with ourselves.

As stated, when we scapegoat, it is usually an unconscious act but when we become conscious of doing so it serves as a reminder of how we use projection to purposely blind ourselves to our own character traits and to absolve ourselves of any responsibility for what we see in our world that we do not like and judge to be wrong.

Eliminating judgment and blame begins with altering our perception of "the other". Can we see the other, including groups and other collectives, no matter where they are along the spectrum of consciousness, as part of us, as part of our One Self and reach out in a spirit of understanding and universal familial love?

CREATING DRAMA CANNOT BRING US PEACE

Personal drama is ego-based. It is when someone exaggerates a situation to get attention. Drama inflates a person or situation to be bigger or worse than they are, so leads away from what is the truth of oneself, a person, or situation.

When we see an actor in a movie, we sometimes project character traits onto what this person is like in real life. We often do the same with politicians and celebrities. Even though we don't know them, we imagine how they might be. In our everyday lives, we do the same with the people around us. Perceiving ourselves to be separate from others, we often project characteristics onto them believing this is who they are. When we project, life's passing scenes in our story can take on the appearance of a drama. This happens because projection feeds our egoic perpetrator, victim, and victor roles and the struggle that ensues between them.

An interesting observation is that many people, if not most, who are drawn to creating and responding to outward drama are living vicariously through drama because they don't have a vibrant, captivating inner life.

On an everyday personal level, before you can correct your

perceptions and end the drama, you first need to own your projections. Suppose something distresses you. You would likely not be in distress were projection not occurring. Whenever you are experiencing anything less than peace between yourself and another person, projection is often at work. Instead of seeing the person as they really are and accepting them as they are, you are putting your own exaggerated negativity or sense of aggrandizement onto them—projecting an aspect of your egoic self "out there," instead of facing up to the reality of it being within you.

We can see people as they are - recognizing their flaws without personally judging them. This is perfectly alright. We recognize what is fact, but by not judging through projection, we are more likely to maintain our peace.

If you drop judgment and be present in life, what do you really see when you look at another person or a situation? What do you actually experience about them when you encounter them in life and experience them free of your conditioned fear-based projections? Does this not remind you about what we covered earlier regarding Mindfulness? When we come from being free of the screen of conditioned thinking, free of our judgments and projections, life becomes far less dramatic but simpler and more peaceful.

PRACTICE
Are there areas in your life that you exaggerate to get attention? If so, identify them. What "benefit" do you get out of them? Try to stop them.

FROM PARTICIPATING IN DRAMA TO WITNESSING IT

When we blindly participate in drama, meaning when we *become* the protagonist in our own drama or a supporting role in someone else's, we lose ourselves in that role. We are then no longer conscious that we are playing a part. When this happens, it can be difficult to access anything outside of it. As the protagonist or member of the supporting cast, we become removed from reality.

To help us break out of our dramas, many spiritual traditions advise that we cultivate the practice of self-observation or what has been referred to as "witnessing" ourselves. This requires a deliberate intention to break free from identification with our dramatic roles. By becoming a witness to these roles we play, we break identification with them and bring in another level of awareness.

When we witness ourselves, we come to see that there are at least two levels of consciousness—identification with the role and the witness of the player of the role. From the position of the witness, we can see things that we are blind to when we are fully identified with our role. We can also then better see ourselves as others see us. We can observe our dysfunctional ego at work. We can identify motives we keep hidden from ourselves when we play our dramatic roles. Witnessing ourselves is powerful because through it we start to experience that we are not at all times who we think we are.

The perception shifts that come with being able to witness ourselves are from "I am only this role that I am playing" to "I am not this role I am playing"; from "I believe human drama is important" to "This is not that important."

Is there something beyond the witnessing state? Yes. This is the state of pure Being. The further shift is from even the limited identification with the observer to the realization we are the unlimited expression of our Source. This new state of Self-awareness is a shift from identification with separation and the feeling, "I am alone" to a realization of Oneness and a knowing "I am not alone." It is a movement from observing life, to realizing we are not separate from Life—we *are* Life.

When you experience drama in your personal life, do you feed it and keep it going? When you begin to witness your own drama, you are able to bring to this illusory form of life the essence of your true Self. When you witness yourself being selfish, you are then free to choose to be generous. When you witness yourself reacting to your children in anger, you can choose to remain peaceful when their behavior is aggravating. When you are falsely accused by your neighbor, instead of reacting to the false accusation, you can stand your ground in stillness and peace, bringing an end to the drama—at least for yourself. When you notice that you have thrown yourself into the pit of martyrs, you can correct your perception and remind yourself that your true Self cannot be a victim of anyone or any circumstance, although there are some circumstances we cannot control or stop.

When you see your sisters and brothers caught up in their dramas, you can assist them to break out of them by not entering them yourself. Be the silent witness to their dramas. Don't buy into their stories to vicariously get an energetic jolt, whether positive or negative. Don't participate in or encourage their ego-centric self-aggrandizing, poor me storytelling, or gossip.

Most of what we read in the newspapers and see on the television news is drama that affects us on a collective scale. Note the same perpetrator, victim, and victor roles being played. Be vigilant so as not to be drawn into the endless and mostly disturbing collective drama on the world scene. As a society, we are so hungry for drama on both the personal and collective levels that we may blindly perpetuate it against our best interests on both levels. Many of us have become so addicted to drama that, at times, we seem to want it to continue even when it becomes harmful to our health. The combination of this addiction and our modern technologies could lead us to an awareness that we have pushed things beyond any semblance of sanity and control.

When reading events in the newspaper or watching them unfold on television, note the facts but don't enter into the drama. Feel the appropriate response to the situation. See the event for what it is, but don't get caught up in the human drama and speculate on possible outcomes. Avoid the commentary from the pundits, most of whom have been chosen as experts but usually fuel separation. They are being set-up to foster the on-going drama of opposite opinions which further fosters not wisdom but polarity.

BEING VERSUS DRAMA

When we don't know who we truly are, we make up stories about ourselves in the hope of finding ourselves. In these dramas, we are the protagonist and all others are our supporting cast.

When we are deadened to our spiritual life, we tend to create drama for ourselves in order to experience some semblance of excitement, even if this works against us. Our stories are a means of feeling that something "important" is happening.

If you listen to your own stories, you will see the predominant themes running through them are either that of victim or victor. The self-indulgent ego relishes both roles—if it can't play one, it will happily play the other. We welcome the opportunity to tell others about our achievements and our pain, especially our pain.

Note what happens when you drop the role of either victor or victim. Where is the separation then? This applies to when we look at others too. What if you looked at the disheveled homeless person and did not see a victim, someone to pity or feel guilty about? What if you did the same with the woman dying of cancer or the injured soldier? What would you see then? How would you act toward them then?

When we can't manufacture enough stories in our own life, we tend to also live vicariously through the drama of others. We turn to soap operas, reality television shows, and gossip. Indeed, the media in North America and other parts of the world is little other than a storybook of egoic dramas. How people love to write about or to get in front of the camera and tell their stories, particularly those sad stories that justify their victim roles of poor me or how I overcame poor me and now am victorious me.

Your stories are made up of past events in chronological order. The egoic mind's habitual pattern is to go back and forth along this life line of events and look for a place to reactivate something by bringing the past into the present, and often by picking at our emotional wounds and regrets. The victim and victor cannot exist without the past. Try dropping your sad story and you will drop your pain. Drop aggrandizing yourself to get attention and you will feel worthy of others' honest attention and appreciation. Drop your most recent story of who did what to you yesterday and you will be more prone to live in the present moment.

If you feel any dissonance, angst, resentment, worry, in short, if you are experiencing any emotional or psychological pain—try stepping out of your story. Just do it. Step out. Drop the past. Don't go to the event or series of events from which that part of the "story of you" is derived. What will be left will be some residual uncomfortable feeling that will soon fade away. The pain or discomfort cannot survive without the story. If the mind comes in and tries to start the story once more, simply say to yourself, "Mind, be still. I am not my story." Keep saying this until you are convinced of this truth.

You can spend your whole life entangled in your dramatic story by often repeating the same scenarios over and over again. Actually, when you look at the stories we tell ourselves, you will notice that there are not that many stories out there. I've made it, you haven't. I am the greatest. I am unlucky. I have been abandoned. No one appreciates me. I am suffering an illness. Different casts, but the same familiar stories. Observe yourself. See what stories you tell yourself or tell others. Notice how you hang on to your drama even if it brings you pain because it is a way of drawing attention to yourself and therefore feeling you are important, you matter to someone. Many will enjoy being drawn into your dramatic story because it vicariously feeds what I call their "drama body".

ASSUMPTIONS FEED DRAMA

A more subtle way we create drama is through making assumptions. Such assumptions can be a disguised form of judgment. These often become the basis of intentional gossip.

We create a lot of internal drama in our lives by dwelling on possible fearful aspects of life: the challenges that will come with inevitable aging, things that might go wrong to prevent the holiday from going smoothly, or the consequences of a downturn in the stock market. You can put yourself in a state of paranoia without any basis whatsoever based just on fearful speculations.

I heard of a woman who, when she was about to enter her neighborhood grocery store, noticed a young homeless person sitting on the pavement. The scene touched her heart. "He is someone's beloved son," she told herself. While shopping, she picked up a gourmet chocolate chip cookie to give him on her way out.

Leaving the store, she leaned down to hand the cookie to him. She was surprised when, instead of taking it immediately, he asked, "Does it have chocolate in it?"

"Yes, it does," she confirmed.

"Then, no thank you," said the young lad.

She was very put off by this youngster. Here he was on the street, supposedly hungry, yet he could turn down her generous offering. Grrrr.

A few weeks later, shopping at the same grocery store and still incensed about the young man, she couldn't help but relate the incident to the woman at the checkout counter. "Oh," said the clerk, "his name is Ivan. He is highly allergic to chocolate."

She collapsed inside with shame for assuming Ivan was just being picky and ungrateful.

Surely all of us can recount times when we too made negative assumptions that proved to be untrue and how self-incriminating we felt after.

Any psychologist or conflict resolution professional will tell you how much pain is caused by individuals making baseless assumptions and then acting on them as if they were true.

Assumptions are born out of our inability to live with uncertainty. Therefore, we fabricate things in our mind to answer the small and larger unknowns we encounter in life. We want to know, to be certain. This is born out of egoic fear that creates a need to be safe in the world.

When we tell ourselves a story that causes us emotional or psychological pain, why do we hang onto it? What would we feel like if we just dropped it? Then why don't we? When we drop drama from our lives, we experience a more peaceful life and discover a whole new level of energy. Keeping the drama going is draining.

When you choose to drop speculative drama, you will find life is so much more peaceful. Drop the desire to find a way to get even with the thief who broke into your home and you will find peace. Do what you can to stop imagining possible results of the risk-taking behavior of your teenage son so that this won't be disguised as anger and thereby interfere with your ability to show him your love. Try to limit your concern over a pending surgery and you will be more likely to continue to enjoy each moment of your life in the meantime - and deal with the surgery when it becomes a reality, instead of for weeks before. Recognizing such are difficult challenges, we can only try to do the best we can when we encounter them. Conscious preparedness through spiritual practice is our greatest support.

Animals are beautiful mirrors for how we can respond to life without holding onto drama. A number of years ago, my aged dog was showing signs of declining health through a weakened immune system, which made him vulnerable to numerous serious infections. In his simple animal nature, he didn't identify with his illness as if it defined him. He didn't create a drama around it. Maintaining his sweet doggie devotion, he continued to express the joy of simply being alive. In so many ways our pets, our hairy and wooly "angels" are amongst our greatest teachers.

PRACTICE
Recall a few times when you made assumptions of others, later to find out they were erroneous. Do you recall the process you went through before making the assumptions or did you just make them automatically? What was the outcome of each assumption in terms of how it affected your relationship with the person?

19

WHERE ARE WE NOW?

The journey to higher and higher consciousness is endless.
However, as we come to the end of this book, it bears asking
ourselves, "Where are we now?" Are we feeling more hopeful, more
peaceful? Do we have some awareness of what we need to do to
bring ourselves inner peace? Do we now know what impedes our
inner peace and how to go beyond these impediments? Have we
come to a better understanding of who we truly are, the One Self?
Has our doing the Practices helped us move into a more peaceful
way of being?

Anything that is not of peace is not of our true Self. To move into
an abiding state of peace takes as long as it takes. The good news
is that we have likely already made significant progress by reading
this book. In addition, we now know what to do to accelerate that
progress with the new awareness we have acquired.

At times we will feel the quiet bliss of peace. At other times, this
inner peace will elude us. This is to be expected. It is challenging

to be predominately peaceful when those we love are suffering and we look outside of ourselves and not see a peaceful world. Now we know we need to heal ourselves in order to be of greater service to others, and to help heal our world so we experience world peace, we need to extend our inner peace to others.

We may feel the need to come back to certain parts of this book many times to remind ourselves of such things as what the ego is, how we can recognize when we are coming from our false egoic-self, how to break free of it, how to deal with the pain from the past we still hold within the body, and so on.

Let's remember our human body holds universal intelligence and to go within through silent prayer or meditation to tap into this supportive, healing, aiding intelligence. And let's live in gratitude for this. Practice meditation as a way of life. There is no greater power than this, since in this way we can access the wisdom of our Source and Its attributes. In addition, there is no better way to come into the realization that we are one with our Source, than by sharing Its attributes.

When we are in "wobble", let's talk to trusted family or friends about how we are feeling, and without going into victimhood, share our inner world. Likely they are feeling or have felt the same or similar to the way we are feeling at the time. Such sharing helps both parties. Such sharing creates bonding and brings us closer to the realization of our Oneness. It is also relieving to know we are not alone in our human challenges.

Let's "cultivate our own garden", meaning let's focus on creating and improving our own smaller world, bringing more peace to our relationships and situations by doing what we can to make them more positive, harmonious, loving.

There are several things we can do quickly when we feel we have lost our peace:

- BREATHE. When you feel anxious or off balance, an effective way to get back to inner harmony is to take deep breaths from the belly to the upper chest, then let the breath out as slowly as you can. You can do this more easily if you put your lips together in a whistle position, then let the breath release. Keep doing this until you feel you are relaxed and centered again.
- When negative energy from the past or fear-based energy regarding the future want to pull you in, let it come and pass on through you.
- Bring yourself back to the present moment and notice that in this present moment there is almost always peace. Do this as many times a day as you feel the need to do so.
- Remember when you feel any form of fear, realize it is the ego at work and don't let yourself be taken in and become its hostage.
- If you can, stop doing anything that does not bring you peace.
- Extend deserved compliments liberally, thus reminding your brothers and sisters of their worth, their value. By doing this, you reinforce your own worth and gain inner strength.
- Give appreciation and thanksgiving often. This raises your vibrational level, bringing you to a higher state of consciousness.
- Light a candle and remind yourself you *are* the Light.
- Have fun, thereby reminding yourself of the joy of your true Being.
- Have a cup of soothing tea.

20

ALL AFFECTS ALL

Both the mystics throughout the ages and now quantum science, confirm that all is joined with all and so all affects all, regardless of time and space that may appear to separate us. Everyone reading this book now, those who have read it in the past, and those who will read it in the future will have all taken this journey together. Hopefully we now feel connected in our Oneness and formed our own community of peace lovers and peace bringers. As more come to read this book, our community will grow and through that our support and sense of Oneness will grow. As some or many readers achieve greater inner peace, this will assist all readers to experience the same. And because all affects all, non-readers as well.

In this way, there is the possibility we can reach the critical mass required to bring us lasting inner peace and peace to our world.

Blessings to you all & Namasté.

ACKNOWLEDGEMENTS

I would like to thank my wonderful editor and dear friend Shirley Spaxman for working in tandem with me as I wrote this book. She has both the editorial skills and spiritual awareness required to have accompanied me on this literary undertaking. Both of our love and noble intention are poured into this book.

Thank you to all those who agreed to be early peer reviewers of the draft of this book and provide valuable feedback on how it could be further improved: Victoria Ritchie, Vim Rolaff, Melisa Dzamastagic, and Catherine Chiesa.

Thank you to Mary Kellough, my amazing and highly gifted daughter, for supporting me with her insight, wise counsel and love while writing this.

Most importantly, I want to thank my beloved husband Howard whose faith in me and ongoing support have provided an unshakable foundation upon which I have been able to take the steps required to face life's challenges and opportunities with courage—however questionable or wobbly this courage has been at times.

NOTES

CHAPTER 2
1. See https://4ocean.com
2. Hopi Elders' Prophesy, Oraibi, Arizona, Hopi Nation, June 8, 2000.

CHAPTER 3
1. See https://tlexinstitute.com/how-to-effortlessly-have-more-positive-thoughts. Reference the 2005 National Science Foundation study.
2. Poetry excerpts from the *Dhammapada*, 42-43.
3. Libby Copeland, "Why Mind Wandering Can Be So Miserable, According to the Happiness Experts", SmithsonianMag.com, February 24, 2017.
4. See https://eliseballard.com/2013/01/29/deepak-chopras-greatest-epiphany-in-life-as-told-to-elise-ballard/ See also Elise Ballard, *Epiphany - True Stories of Sudden Insight to Inspire, Encourage, and Transform*, New York, Harmony Books, 2014.

CHAPTER 5
1. Psalm 46:10 King James Version (KJV), Public Domain.
2. John 8:7 King James Version (KJV), Public Domain.
3. Proverbs 29:18 King James Version (KJV), Public Domain.

CHAPTER 6
1. Martin Luther King Jr., Speech to the Southern Christian Leadership Conference, Atlanta, Georgia, August 16, 1967.

CHAPTER 7
1. Luke 17:21 King James Version (KJV), Public Domain.
2. Study on the Maharishi Effect. Can group meditation lower crime rate and violence? See https://tmhome.com/benefits/study-maharishi-effect-group-meditation-crime-rate/
3. 1 Percent Effect/Transcendental Meditation. See https://www.tm.org/blog/marharishi/maharishi-on-the-1-effect/
4. Linda Sechrist, "A Global Wake-Up Call - Collective Consciousness Nears Spiritual Tipping Point." Retrieved from internet: natural awakenings magazine - global wake-up-call.

CHAPTER 8
1. Barry Long, *Stillness is the Way*, New South Wales, Australia: Barry Long Books, 1989, 10.

CHAPTER 10
1. See "Sensing Your Spirit body - Swedenborg and Life" - YouTube. See also Emanuel Swedenborg, *Secrets of Heaven*, Vol. 1 and 2, New Century Edition, trans. Lisa Hyatt Cooper, West Chester, PA: Swedenborg Foundation, 2008, 10199.

2. Joseph McMoneagle, *Memoirs of a Psychic Spy*, Charlottesville, VA: Hampton Roads Publishing, 2002.
3. Dr. Joy Martina, "Why Science is Calling the Heart Your Second Brain." See website christallin.com>science-calling-heart-second-brain
4. Ibid
5. The Quick Coherence Technique for Adults, HeartMath Institute. See https:www.heartmath.org/resources/heartmath-tools/quick-coherence-technique-for-adults
6. "The Three Brains: How to Awaken Your 3 Intelligence Centers." See calmwithyoga.com

CHAPTER 11
1. Ivan Rados, *Health - It's All About Consciousness*, Vancouver, Canada: Namaste Publishing, 2009, 154-155.
2. James L. Oschman, *Energy Medicine: The Scientific Basis*, 2nd ed., Milton, Ontario, Canada: Elsevier, October 2015. See also Cyndi Dale, "A Complete Guide to the Human Energy Fields and Etheric Bodies." consciouslifestylemag.com
3. "Do Cells Have Intelligence?" See www.basic.northwestern.edu.g-buehler
4. Ibid.
5. Dr. Pradipta Ghosh, "Decoding Cellular Intelligence" - Ted Talk, Dec. 4, 2018.

CHAPTER 12
1. Dr. David Berceli, *The Revolutionary Trauma Release Process*, Vancouver, Canada: Namaste, Sept. 2008, 89-91.
2. Foundation for Inner Peace, *Concordance of A Course In Miracles*, c-in-2:5, New York: Penguin Group, 1997.

CHAPTER 14
1. Film documentary "Water - The Great Mystery - Explore the Power of Consciousness," DVD, produced by Saida Medvedeva, Sergey Shumakov, Vasiliy Anisimov, distributed by Voice Entertainment in Association with Masterskaya Productions, 2006.
2. Ibid.
3. Ibid.
4. Ibid.

CHAPTER 17
1. Matthew 18:22, King James Version (KJV), Public Domain.
2. Michael Brown, *The Presence Process*, revised edition, Vancouver, Canada: Namaste, 2010.

CHAPTER 18
1. Foundation for Inner Peace, *Concordance of A Course In Miracles*, t-26 ix.6:1, New York: Penguin Group, 1997.

BIBLIOGRAPHY

Berceli, David. *The Revolutionary Trauma Release Process*. Vancouver, Canada: Namaste Publishing, 2008.

Braden, Gregg. *Resilience from the Heart*. Carlsbad, California: Hay House, 2015.

Brown, Michael. *The Presence Process: A Journey into Present Moment Awareness*. Vancouver, Canada: Namaste Publishing, 2010.

Kellough, Constance. *The Leap – Are You Ready to Live a New Reality?* (No longer in print). Vancouver, Canada: Namaste Publishing, 2007.

Long, Barry. *Stillness Is the Way*. London, England: Barry Long Books, 1996.

Rados, Ivan. *Health: It's All About Consciousness*. Vancouver, Canada: Namaste Publishing, 2009.

The Foundation for Inner Peace. *A Course in Miracles*. Glen Ellen, California, 1990.

Tolle, Eckhart. *The Power of Now*. Vancouver, Canada: Namaste Publishing, 1998.

Tolle, Eckhart. *A New Earth: Awakening to Your Life's Purpose*. Penguin Books (This is a Namaste Publishing Book licensed to Penguin Books.) New York, New York: Penguin Books, 2005.

ADDITIONAL RECOMMENDED READING

Barrett, Sondra. *Secrets of Your Cells – Discovering Your Body's Inner Intelligence.* Boulder, Colorado: Sounds True, 2013.

Frankl, Viktor E. *Man's Search for Meaning.* Amazon.com, Kindle Edition, (n.d.)

Goldsmith, Joel R. *Living the Infinite Way.* Santa Barbara, California: Acropolis Books, 1961.

Levine, Peter A. *Healing Trauma: A Pioneering Program for Restoring the Wisdom of the Body.* Boulder, CO: Sounds True, 2008.

Levine, Peter A. and Ann Frederick. *Waking the Tiger: Healing Trauma.* Berkley, California: North Atlantic Books, 1997.

Lipton, Bruce H. *The Biology of Belief – Unleashing the Power of Consciousness, Matter & Miracles.* Carlsbad, California: Hay House, 2005.

McTaggart, Lynn. *The Field – The Quest for the Secret Force of the Universe.* New York, New York: Harper, 2008.

Mendes, Joao & Mendes Ramiro. Sound – *The Fabric of Soul, Consciousness, Reality, and the Cosmos.* Cheyenne, WY: Quantum World Enterprise, 2015.

APPENDIX A

For those who have practiced the Innerbody Meditation in Chapter 8 and have become familiar with it, the following is a shorter version. Once you have become practiced at entering the inner body, you can ignite the energy of consciousness in just a few parts of the body to take attention away from the thinking mind and continue to awaken the consciousness in the body.

Set up for this meditation as you have been guided to do. Make sure you are breathing naturally and become conscious of your breath. Now ignite the energy in one hand, then the other; one foot, then the other. While still feeling your breath, also ignite the inner energy of your shoulder area. Feel the sensation from shoulder to shoulder, making sure your shoulders are relaxed when you do so. Now ignite the energy in your upper then lower arms. Hold to the sensation in all these areas at the same time. Notice if the consciousness in the body wants to awaken in other areas as well. You will know this if you feel sensation in another part or parts of your body without even putting your attention there. Stay in your inner body for 5-10 minutes.

APPENDIX B

Questions to ask yourself after you have drawn your life line as stated in the Practice on page 124.

1. Does my life line include only facts and events, or does it also indicate my personal growth and spiritual turning point experiences?

2. Has most of my life been lived being ego-centered and identifying myself solely with my body and thinking mind?

3. Do I notice any repetitive patterns? If so, what are they and the reasons for each?

4. Do I mention only the good pivotal events of my life and not those that caused me worry or suffering?

5. Which things in my life have given me the greatest contentment, joy, sense of purpose?

6. Did I have periods in my life when I was clearly of service to another or others? If so, did I mention these? If so, what was the nature of my service to another or others?

7. Does my life line indicate growth in character and awareness as I grew older? If so, what were the catalysts for such growth? Certain teachers, events, life challenges, people who were in or entered my life?

8. What gifts or special talents does my life line indicate?

9. Does it indicate areas of my uniqueness?

10. Based on the above questions and my answers, I can now add any additional information to my life line that I have become aware of as a result.

11. What would I like to add to my life line 2 years out? 5 years out? Why?

12. Looking at my life line and extended projected life line, does a service intent become evident that is something I am able to and want to do now? Later? If not, am I willing to go into my heart and hold to the intent that in time it does become evident to me?

If you enjoyed this book, you may also love...

THE
CHRONICLES
OF

A
STUDENT OF TRUTH

An illustrated book of short, sweet, inspirational stories
by Constance Kellough, author of
The HOW to Inner Peace

books that change your life

namaste

PUBLISHING

Our Publishing Mission is to make available healing
and transformational publications that acknowledge,
celebrate, and encourage our readers to live from their
true essence and thereby come to remember
who they truly are.

STAY INSPIRED.

WWW.NAMASTEPUBLISHING.COM

@NAMASTEBOOKS

NOTES